The Contented
Little Baby
Book of Weaning

The Contented Little Baby Book of Weaning

Your one-stop guide to contented feeding

Gina Ford

Vermilion
LONDON

First published in the United Kingdom in 2002 by Vermilion, an imprint of Ebury Press
Random House UK Ltd
Random House
20 Vauxhall Bridge Road
London SW1V 2SA

Random House Australia (Pty) Limited
20 Alfred Street, Milsons Point, Sydney,
New South Wales 2061, Australia

Random House New Zealand Limited
18 Poland Road, Glenfield, Auckland 10, New Zealand

Random House (Pty) Limited
Endulini, 5A Jubilee Road, Parktown 2193, South Africa

Random House UK Limited Reg. No. 954009
www.randomhouse.co.uk

Papers used by Vermilion are natural recyclable products made from wood grown in sustainable forests.

A CIP catalogue record for this book is available from the British Library

ISBN: 0 09 187663 X

Printed and bound in Great Britain by
Mackays of Chatham plc, Chatham, Kent

Contents

For my god-daughter Brontë Sherbourne,
a very special and contented baby.

Acknowledgements

I would like to express my thanks and gratitude to the hundreds of parents who I have worked with or advised over the years. Their constant feedback on their children's eating habits has been an enormous help in writing this book. In particular I would like to say a special thank you to Françoise and Steven Skelly – parents of Isabella and Oliver; Helen and David Sherbourne – parents of Alexander and Brontë; Juliette and Alistair Scott – parents of Samantha and Poppy; and Julie and Alvin Stardust – parents of Milly.

A special thank you to my Aunt Jean, Uncle Dan and my cousins Ann Clough, Helen Ramsay and Sheila Eskdale for your love, continued support and encouragement and for helping look after my darling Molly. I would also like to thank Jane Revell, Carla Fodden Flint and Sandra Gregory for the special friendship and emotional support you have given me. Thank you also to the Reverend Tony Adamson and family for your friendship, emotional support and spiritual guidance, and for not giving up on trying to save my soul!

The Bradford Leisure Club in Northumberland deserves a special mention as it became my little piece of heaven here on earth, while writing this book. Thank you to Lance Robson and all the staff for your support and encouragement in my attempt to get fit while writing this book. To my dear friend and fantastic personal trainer Robert Redpath for not giving up on me – either physically or *mentally*, and to his wife Sonia, for all her support and wise advice – particularly on bad hair days!

A very special debt of thanks to my agent Emma Todd for her enormous help, support and encouragement during the last year. Also to everyone at Random House, in particular to Fiona MacIntyre and editors Lesley McOwan and Miren Lopategui. I am eternally grateful for your never-ending support and endless patience. My thanks, too, to Sara Lewis and Emma-Lee Gow for their help with compiling the recipes and to Paul Sacher, specialist clinical dietician, for his valuable contributions to the book. Becky Bagnell, mother of Seymour aged 18 months, a true contented little baby, also deserves a huge thank you for helping me with my manuscripts and in getting my message across about CLB.

As always I am eternally grateful for the huge support I receive from the thousands of readers of my books who take the time to phone and write to me – a huge thank you to you all and much love to your contented babies.

Finally, I would like to say a very special and loving thank you to my darling Molly for bringing so much love and laughter back into my life and for being such a good baby during the writing of this book. She is living proof that even a baby boxer is happier following the CLB routines!

Introduction

If you want to establish long-term healthy eating habits for your baby, it is important to put a lot of thought into the early stages of weaning – not only into how much your baby eats, but also when and what he eats. I believe that how and when a baby is introduced to solids, along with the type of food offered, plays a huge part in determining his future eating habits.

In my second book, *From Contented Baby to Confident Child: Problem-Solving in the First Three Years*, I said I believed that a great many parents were struggling to meet the current guidelines on healthy feeding – the advice being to start introducing solids to babies between the ages of four and six months, and to establish a pattern of three proper meals a day between the age of six and nine months.

By the age of one year, the theory goes, a baby is expected to be eating much the same food as the rest of the family. Sadly, however, for a large number of parents this is not the case and a great many find that by the time their baby reaches toddlerhood, mealtimes have become a battlefield involving much cajoling, tears and tantrums as worried parents try to persuade their children to eat small amounts of healthy food. According to numerous newspaper and magazine reports, our children's diet in the 2000s is worse than it was in the 1950s, and a large number of teenagers are facing a great many serious health problems as a result of unhealthy eating habits in early life.

Judging by the ever-rising numbers of anxious parents who contact me about their children's eating problems, I believe this problem has not been exaggerated. I am more convinced than ever that the root of a great many of the feeding difficulties experienced by parents today stems from milk feeding in the early days. A lack of structure in the way this is organised can often lead to a baby drinking either too much, which can result in his refusing solids, or too little, which can make him increase his solid intake too quickly, thereby depriving him of the vital nutrients offered by milk.

The first baby I helped care for – more than 20 years ago – was weaned on to baby rice at the age of ten weeks. This was fairly common at the time. Baby food manufacturers promoted weaning from the age of three months, and for parents of unsettled babies weaning slightly earlier than this often seemed the answer. Today, although the recommended age for weaning has changed, I find the attitude of many parents much the same as it was many years ago: an unsettled baby is a hungry baby. Despite the enormous research which proves that weaning too early can cause long-term health problems, many parents continue to introduce solids long before the recommended age of four months.

My aim in this book is to help to guide you through this important phase in you and your baby's lives. Each chapter deals with a different stage of weaning, with simple guidelines to help you through. There are also stage-by-stage feeding plans and recipes, which I hope you will find useful. In essence, the book is a guide to weaning, and the recipes are there to help parents and to give ideas for their baby's meals, but there are many other books on the market that give excellent meal suggestions (see Further Reading). It may be worth investigating a few. Remember, time (and money) invested in the early months will pay dividends in the long run.

When to Wean

1

The current advice is that babies should be weaned somewhere between four and six months of age. Up to the age of six months milk is still the most important baby food, providing a perfect balance of nutrients, vitamins and minerals. It is important, therefore, to remember that any solids you introduce to your baby at this stage will only be to get him used to different tastes. Building up the amount of solids your baby takes should be done over many weeks. The 1994 report by the Committee on Medical Aspects of Food Policy (COMA) entitled 'Weaning and the Weaning Diet' advises that parents introducing solids too early or increasing the amount too quickly could result in some, if not all, of the following:

- Possible damage to the baby's digestive system. It takes up to four months for the lining of a baby's gut to develop and for the kidneys to mature enough to cope with the waste products from solid food. Introducing solids before your baby has a complete set of enzymes required to digest food properly could put pressure on his liver and kidneys and impair his digestive system.

- Physical problems when feeding. It is important not to start weaning before the baby's neuromuscular co-ordination has developed enough for him to control his head and neck while sitting upright supported in a chair to be fed. He should also be able to swallow food easily, by moving it from the front of his mouth to the back. He will only be able to do this if he is supported upright.

- Introducing solids too early can put your baby at a higher risk of developing allergic conditions such as asthma, eczema and hay fever.

- According to COMA, scientific studies in Scotland found that a persistent cough was more common in babies who had been given solids before 12 weeks.

- A baby who is given solids too soon or increases them too rapidly may cut back too much on his milk and be denied the essential nutrients that milk provides.

- Early weaning can sometimes lead to overfeeding, making the baby too fat, which, research suggests, can lead to obesity in later life and increase the risk of cancer, diabetes, heart disease, etc.

In accordance with the advice given in the COMA report and my own personal experience I hope the following guidelines will help you to decide if your baby is ready to be weaned. Your baby will be ready for weaning if:

- He is four months old.

- He has been taking a full feed four or five times a day from both breasts or a 240ml (8oz) formula feed and has been happily going for four hours between feeds, but now gets irritable and chews his hands long before his next feed is due.

- He has been taking a full feed from both breasts or a 240ml (8oz) formula feed and screams for more the minute the feed finishes.

- He usually sleeps well at night and nap times, but is starting to wake up earlier and earlier.

- He is chewing his hands excessively, displaying eye to hand co-ordination and trying to put things into his mouth.

If your baby is four months old, has doubled his birth weight and is constantly showing most of the above signs, he is probably ready to begin weaning. As with weaning too soon, delaying weaning when a baby is giving all the signals of being ready for solids can also create problems. Research carried out by clinical psychologist Gillian Harris found that babies who were introduced to a wide range of non-allergy-forming foods between the ages of four and six months accepted a wider range of foods at one year than those weaned on a restricted diet. I agree with this, as I have found that parents who miss this window of opportunity for weaning end up feeding their babies excessive quantities of milk, which results in their babies refusing most solids and becoming very fussy eaters.

Establishing a feeding schedule

If your baby is not already established on a milk-feeding schedule I would strongly advise you to try to establish some sort of structure before you begin weaning. For further information please refer to *The New Contented Little Baby Book* also published by Vermilion.

A baby on a structured milk feeding plan would gradually go from milk feeding to a balanced diet of three meals a day by one year of age.

During the first stage of weaning, though, it is important to remember that milk is still the most important food, as it provides your baby with the right balance of vitamins and minerals. Solids at this stage are only classed as 'first tastes' and fillers, which should be increased very slowly over several weeks, gradually preparing your baby for three solid meals a day. By always offering the milk feed first, you will ensure that his daily milk intake does not decrease too rapidly during the first months of weaning.

Which foods?

During the first year babies grow rapidly, and most will have tripled their birth weight by the time they reach their first birthday. To ensure that your baby grows at the right rate, develops strong bones and teeth, firm muscles and healthy tissues it is essential that the food you give him has the right balance of nutrients.

The following section divides food into the five different food groups. By giving your baby the recommended daily number of servings from each group shown, you can be sure that his daily nutritional needs are being met.

FOOD GROUPS FOR A NUTRITIONALLY ADEQUATE DIET

Group One: Milk, Dairy Products and Substitutes

Breast milk, infant formula, cow's milk, lassi, yoghurt, fromage frais, cottage cheese, hard cheese, infant soya formula, tofu.

Major nutrients
Energy (calories) and fat. Protein, calcium, vitamin A, B vitamins, zinc. Iron and vitamin D in breast and formula milks.

4–6 months
Minimum of 600ml (20oz) of breast milk or formula, inclusive of milk used in solids such as yoghurt.

6–9 months
Minimum of 500–600ml (16–20oz) of breast, formula or follow-on milk, inclusive of milk used in solids. Hard cheese can be used in sauces; also cubed, grated and as a finger food.

9–12 months
Minimum of 500–600ml (16–20oz) of breast milk, formula milk or follow-on milk, inclusive of milk used in solids.

After one year
Minimum of 350ml (12oz) of full-fat cow's milk (or suitable alternative e.g. formula or calcium enriched soya milk), inclusive

of milk used in solids, or two servings of dairy products. If milk drinks are rejected, use alternatives such as cheese, yoghurts, etc.

- Discourage large volumes (more than 600ml/20oz) of milk after one year, as it will stop the appetite for other foods.

- Discourage feeding from the bottle after one year.

Group Two: Carbohydrates

Bread, rolls, baby cereals, fortified breakfast cereals, oats and other cereals, plain and savoury biscuits, potatoes, yams, millet, pasta, semolina, rice.

Major nutrients

Energy (calories). Thiamine, niacin, folic acid, vitamin B_6, biotin, zinc, fibre.

4–6 months (first tastes)

Introduce small amounts of gluten-free low-fibre (e.g. rice-based) baby cereal and finely mashed or puréed starchy vegetables such as potatoes, sweet potatoes, yams.

6–9 months (2–3 servings of 2 tbsp each)

Introduce wholemeal bread, pasta and cereals. Foods can have a more solid, 'lumpier' texture. Start giving finger foods such as toast.

9–12 months (3–4 servings)

Encourage wholemeal products; discourage foods with added sugar such as biscuits, cakes, etc. Starchy foods can be of a solid texture.

After one year (minimum of 4 servings daily)

Cereal and bread derived from wholegrains are a richer source of nutrients and fibre than refined cereals. Most baby and breakfast cereals are fortified with iron and B vitamins.

- At least one serving, such as one slice of bread, one small baked potato or one portion of cereal, at each mealtime.
- Discourage high-fat foods such as crisps, savoury snacks and pastry.

Group Three: Vegetables and Fruit

Leafy and green vegetables (cabbage, green beans, peas, broccoli, leeks); root vegetables (carrots, onions, turnips); salad vegetables (tomatoes, cucumber), mushrooms, sweetcorn, marrow; fruit (apples, bananas, peaches, oranges, melons), fruit juices.

Major nutrients

Vitamins A, C and folic acid, fibre plus a host of other health-giving nutrients, e.g. trace elements and minerals, many of which function as antioxidants.

4–6 months (first tastes)

Introduce soft-cooked vegetables and fruit as smooth purées (pages 41–5).

6–9 months (minimum of 2 servings daily)

Introduce raw soft fruit and vegetables such as banana, melon and tomato as finger foods. Cooked vegetables and fruit can have a coarser, mashed texture.

9–12 months (3–4 servings)

Encourage lightly cooked or raw food. Chopped or finger food texture is suitable. Give unsweetened orange juice with meals, especially if the diet is meat-free.

After one year (minimum of 4 servings daily)

Encourage unsweetened fruit if vegetables are rejected. Food can be more solid though some fibrous foods, such as celery and radish, may be difficult to eat. Vegetables may be preferred raw, as in grated carrot and chopped tomato, or you may need to disguise them in soups and stews.

- To improve iron absorption, give some food or drink that contains vitamin C with every meal, e.g. strawberries, kiwi fruit, or a small amount (100ml/4floz) of freshly squeezed orange juice.

Group Four: Meat and Meat Alternatives

Meat, poultry, eggs, fish, lentils, beans, baked beans, groundnuts.

Major nutrients
Energy (calories) and fat. Protein, iron, zinc, B vitamins (B_{12} in animal foods only).

6–9 months (1 serving)
Introduce soft-cooked, puréed or minced meat, fish or pulses. Chopped hard-boiled egg can be used as finger food.

9–12 months (minimum of 1 serving daily)
Minimum of one serving of animal protein needed daily, or two of vegetable protein. In a vegetarian diet use a mixture of different vegetable and starchy foods, e.g. macaroni cheese, dhal and rice.

After one year (minimum 1 serving daily)
Encourage low-fat meat and oily fish (sardine, herring, mackerel). Liver pâté can be used after one year.

- Trim fat from meat.
- Use little or no added fat when cooking foods that already contain fat such as meat.

Group Five: Occasional Foods

Cakes, sweet biscuits, sweetened squash, sweetened desserts and milk drinks, ice cream, cream, sugar, jam, honey, crisps, savoury snacks, fried and fatty foods.

Note: None of these foods is necessary in your baby's diet. They contain a lot of fat, energy, sugar or salt. Try not to use foods from this group every day.

6–9 months

Encourage savoury foods rather than sweet ones.
Fruit juices are not necessary; try to restrict them to meal-times.
Use very diluted pure fruit juice (100ml/4floz).

9–12 months

Use moderate amounts of butter, margarine and small amounts of jam on bread. Avoid salty foods.

After one year

Limit crisps and savoury snacks. Give bread or fruit if hungry between meals. Do not add sugar to drinks. Try to limit soft drinks to meal-times or avoid altogether.

- Encourage a pattern of three meals each day.

- Discourage frequent snacking on fatty or sugary foods.

Organic food

A report issued by the Soil Association in 2001 claimed that organic food is healthier for us because it contains more properties that help the body protect against cell damage and cancer. The report also claimed that organic food has improved levels of minerals and vitamin C.

This report, along with an increasing amount of other research into the benefits of organic food has seen the sale of organic food grow at an average rate of 40 per cent a year since 1995. Despite its increased popularity, however, organic food is still considerably more expensive than the non-organic option, which I'm sure plays a big part in people's choice on whether to go organic or not.

Although the government claims that permitted levels of pesticides used on non-organic crops pose no danger to our health, many scientists and food experts believe that even small amounts of these pesticide residues found in food can be harmful.

My own personal belief is that organic food is not only healthier for us, but it also tastes better. When it comes to babies and young children I believe passionately that it is our duty to give them the purest and best food available, particularly during the first two years of life when the building of their immune system is so dependent upon the food they eat.

I appreciate the extra cost involved for families on a budget but, in my opinion, if a choice has to be made on where to cut back on costs, it should never be on food. A child will not suffer long term from having fewer toys or wearing hand-me-down clothes, but a diet of food grown or reared using artificial fertilisers, pesticides, antibiotics and hormones could affect his immune system for life.

The following information should be helpful when considering whether or not to try and wean your baby on organic food:

- Organic food has to meet a strict set of standards regulated by EU law and governed in the UK by the UK Register of Organic Food Standards (UKROFS). Producers and manufacturers have to keep strict details of production, ingredients, distribution, etc. and all organic food is traceable back to its source.

- Organic fruit and vegetable producers are not permitted to use artificial pesticides, fertilisers and fungicides when growing or storing crops. Research shows that non-organic food can have traces of all these chemicals that cannot be removed by washing.

- Organic farmers must feed their livestock a natural diet so that they grow at a natural pace. Growth promoters are prohibited, as is the routine use of antibiotics.

Commercial baby food

Over the years I have encountered considerable problems with babies who are weaned on commercial baby foods – their taste buds become so accustomed to the bland taste of these processed foods that once they are old enough to participate in family meals they simply refuse. Although the introduction of organic ranges by some manufacturers has brought about an improvement in commercial baby food, it is still no match for the distinct flavours and different textures of home-made food.

I also believe that commercially prepared foods, particularly second-stage meals in jars and tins, do not provide enough calories to sustain the rapid growth of young babies, as they are not as energy-dense as home-cooked meals. I have discovered a significant link between night-time waking and commercial baby food. Many babies who previously slept through the night from two to three months will start to wake up several times a night between six months and one year, but once I advise parents to change their baby's diet to a home-cooked one there is nearly always a huge improvement in the baby's sleeping patterns. Many nutritional experts claim that a baby whose diet consists solely of commercial food will not receive enough of the right calories for healthy growth, which would account for such babies waking up genuinely hungry. For example, a home-made recipe for cauliflower cheese contains cauliflower, flour, butter, milk and cheese. A commercially prepared jar of cauliflower cheese may also contain these ingredients, but in lower amounts, and in addition is more than likely to be bulked out with other fillers such as rice, potato and maltodextrin. (Maltodextrin is a sweet bulking agent, usually derived from potato, corn or rice and used to enhance the artificial flavours in many adult foods. It is also used in the gum on postage stamps and envelopes!) None of these bulking agents adds anything of note to commercial baby foods.

If you want to establish lifelong healthy eating habits for your baby, try to restrict the use of commercially prepared baby meals. The occasional use of organic commercial foods without additives and fillers in conjunction with a variety of home-cooked meals is not a problem, but a diet made up mainly of jars and packets may not only create a fussy feeder, but also cause sleeping problems.

The following guidelines will help you choose the best commercially prepared foods on the market.

- Always check the labels for the list of ingredients, which are listed in order of quantity, the largest quantity always coming first. Avoid anything containing preservatives, artificial colourings, sugar, or fillers such as maltodextrin or water. Watch out for hidden sugars such as fructose, dextrose or sucrose.

- Choose pure baby cereals that are free of sugar, starch and maltodextrin. For babies under six months, cereals should also be gluten-free and not contain ingredients such as eggs, citrus fruits or tomatoes, which can trigger allergies.

- Always check the safety button on the top of jars. If the button is raised or the lid can be removed, do not buy it. Never feed your baby food straight from the jar or can. Put the amount he needs into a bowl and refrigerate the remainder. Carefully follow the manufacturer's guidelines for heating, serving and storing leftovers.

Foods to be avoided

During the first two years of your baby's life, certain foods are best used sparingly, or avoided altogether, as they may be harmful to your baby's health. The two worst culprits in this regard are sugar and salt.

Sugar

During the first year of weaning it is best to avoid adding sugar to any of your baby's food, as it may make him develop a taste for sweet things. A baby's appetite for savoury foods can be seriously affected if he is allowed lots of foods containing sugar or sugar substitutes. But when buying commercial foods these ingredients can be hard to avoid. A survey by the Consumer's Association magazine, *Which?*, tested 420 baby products and reported that 40 per cent contained sugar or fruit juice, or both. When choosing baby cereals or commercial foods check the labels carefully; sugar may be listed as dextrose, fructose, glucose or sucrose. Watch out, too, for syrup or concentrated fruit juice, which are also sometimes used as sweeteners.

Too much sugar in the diet may not only make your baby refuse savoury foods, but can also lead to serious problems such as tooth decay and obesity. Because sugar converts very quickly to energy, babies and children who have too much may become very hyperactive. Products such as baked beans, spaghetti hoops, cornflakes, fish fingers, jam, tomato ketchup, tinned soups and some yoghurts are just a few of the everyday foods that contain hidden sugars, so care should be taken that when your baby reaches toddlerhood, he does not eat these foods in excess. It is also important to check the labels of fruit juices and squashes.

Salt

Children under two years of age should not have salt added to their food – they get all the salt they need from natural sources such as vegetables. Adding salt to a young baby's food can be very dangerous as it can put a strain on his immature kidneys. Research also shows that children who develop a taste for salt early in life may be more prone to heart disease later. When your baby reaches the stage of joining in with family meals, it is important that you do not add salt to the food during cooking. Remove your baby's portion, then add salt for the rest of the family.

As with sugar, many processed foods and commercially prepared meals contain high levels of salt. It is important to check the labels on these foods carefully before giving them to your toddler.

Preparing and cooking food for your baby

Making your own food not only often works out cheaper, but, more importantly, will be of great nutritional benefit to your baby. And it needn't be fiddly or time-consuming if you make up large quantities at a time and store mini meals away in the freezer (pages 41–6). Keep sterilised feeding equipment, ice cube trays and freezerproof containers at the ready and follow the general instructions below.

Sterilised feeding equipment

All feeding equipment should be sterilised for the first six months and bottles and teats for as long as they are used. Sterilise ice cube trays or freezer containers by boiling them in a large saucepan of water for five minutes, or soaking them in sterilising solution for 30 minutes. Use a steam steriliser, if you have one, for small items such as spoons or serving bowls and follow timings recommended in the manufacturer's handbook. Wash cooking utensils as usual in a dishwasher, or rinse handwashed items with boiling water from the kettle.

Packing food for the freezer

- Make sure cooked puréed food is covered as quickly as possible and transfer it to the freezer as soon as it is cool enough.

- Never put warm food into a refrigerator or freezer.

- Check the temperature of your freezer on a freezer thermometer. It should read –18°C. If you don't already have a freezer thermometer they can be bought from good hardware shops or the cookware section in large department stores.

- If using an ice cube tray, fill with puréed food, open-freeze until solid, then pop the cubes out of the tray and into a sterilised plastic box. Non-sterilised items such as plastic bags can be used from six months. Seal well and freeze.

- Label items clearly, adding the date.

- Use foods within six weeks.

- Never refreeze cooked food. Food can only be put back into the freezer if it was originally frozen raw then defrosted and cooked – a raw frozen chicken breast, defrosted, for example, can be frozen as a cooked casserole.

Defrosting tips

Defrost frozen (covered) food in the fridge overnight or leave at room temperature if you forget, transferring it to the fridge as soon as it has defrosted. Make sure it is covered at all times and stand it on a plate to catch any drips. Never speed up defrosting by putting food into warm or hot water. Always use defrosted food within 24 hours.

Reheating tips

- When batch cooking, take out a portion of food for your baby to use now and freeze the rest. Don't be tempted to reheat the entire mixture and then freeze what is left.

- If your baby has only eaten a tiny portion it can be tempting to reheat and serve the leftovers later. Please don't – babies are much more susceptible than adults to food poisoning so get in the habit of throwing leftovers away immediately.

- Reheat foods only once.

First Stage Weaning: four to six months

2

Four to five months

If you feel your baby is showing all the signs of needing to be weaned, I would advise you to start by offering him a very small amount of food after the 11am feed. I always use pure organic baby rice as a first weaning food, mixed with either expressed breast milk or formula. Researchers at the University of Surrey have carried out studies into weaning which show that babies who are fed diets with a high fruit content are more prone to diarrhoea, which leads to slow growth. They, too, advocate the use of baby rice as the best first weaning food, since fruit may not be so well tolerated by the underdeveloped gut of some babies.

After a few days, when your baby is taking a full teaspoon of rice, I would introduce a tiny amount of fruit into the baby rice to make it more palatable. However, during the first month of weaning, as your baby's appetite increases, I would always make sure that I increased the quantities of rice rather than fruit, and that I introduced a variety of non-allergy-forming foods (mainly in the form of vegetables). I am convinced that the reason very few of my babies developed a sweet tooth is because they were given more vegetables than fruit in the early days of weaning.

Daily requirements

During the first stage of weaning it is important to remember that milk is still the most important food for your baby, as it provides him with the right balance of vitamins and minerals. Solids at this stage are classed merely as 'first tastes' and fillers, which should be increased very slowly over several weeks gradually preparing your baby for three solid meals a day. By always offering the milk feed first you will ensure that his daily milk intake does not decrease too rapidly during the first month of weaning.

Weaning guidelines

- Introduce solids after the 11am feed. Prepare everything you need for giving the solids in advance: baby chair, two bibs, two spoons and a clean, fresh damp cloth.

- Start by offering your baby one teaspoonful of pure organic rice mixed to a very smooth consistency using either expressed milk, formula or cool, filtered freshly boiled water.

- Make sure the baby rice is cooled enough before feeding it to your baby. Use a shallow plastic spoon – never a metal one, which can be too sharp or get too hot.

- Some babies need help in learning how to feed from the spoon. By placing the spoon just far enough into his mouth, and bringing the spoon up and out against the roof of his mouth, his upper gums will take the food off, encouraging him to feed.

- Once your baby is established on baby rice at 11am and is tolerating it, give the rice after the 6pm feed instead. When he finishes the 1 teaspoonful you have mixed up for three consecutive days, you can increase the rice by half a teaspoonful.

- Once he is taking two teaspoonfuls of baby rice mixed with milk or water after the 6pm feed, a small amount of pear purée (page 41) can be introduced after the 11am feed. This usually happens between the fourth and sixth day.

• If the baby tolerates the pear purée, transfer it to the 6pm feed. Mixing the purée with baby rice in the evening will make it more palatable and prevent the baby from getting constipated.

• Small amounts of various organic vegetables and fruit can now be introduced after the 11am feed. To prevent your baby from developing a sweet tooth, try to give more vegetables than fruit. At this stage, avoid strong-tasting ones like broccoli or spinach, but, rather, concentrate on the root vegetables listed in the Feeding plan at four to five months (below). These contain natural sugars, they will taste sweeter and blander, and may prove more palatable to your baby.

• Introduce a new food every three or four days, keeping a diary so you can see how your baby reacts to each new food.

• Always be very positive and smile when offering new foods. If your baby spits a food out, it may not mean that he dis-likes it. Remember, this is all very new to him, and different foods will get different reactions. If he positively refuses a food, however, leave it and try again in a week.

• Always offer milk first, as this is still the most important food at this stage in nutritional terms. While appetites do vary, in my experience the majority of babies will be drinking 840–900ml (28–30 oz) of formula a day or four to five full breastfeeds. Provided your baby is happy and thriving, the minimum daily recommended amount of milk required at this age is 600ml (20oz) a day.

Feeding plan at four to five months

This plan should be used as a guide for how to introduce your baby to solids. However, all babies differ and all have likes and dislikes, so don't feel anxious if your child doesn't fit in exactly with the plan.

Foods to introduce

Pure organic baby rice, pear, apple, carrot, sweet potato, potatoes, green beans, courgettes and swede.

Note: A 'cube' is equivalent to approximately one level table-spoon.

Days 1–3

7/7.30am	Breast feed or 180–240ml (6–8oz) of formula milk
11am	Breast feed or 180–240ml (6–8oz) of formula milk
	1 tsp of pure organic baby rice mixed with breast milk, formula or cool boiled water
2/2.30pm	Breast feed or 150–210ml (5–7oz) of formula milk
6pm	Breast feed or 180–240ml (6–8oz) of formula milk
10pm	Breast feed or 150–210ml (5–7oz) of formula milk (optional).

Days 4–6

7/7.30am	Breast feed or 180–240ml (6–8 oz) of formula milk
11am	Breast feed or 180–240ml (6–8oz) formula milk
	1 cube of pear purée (page 41), optional
2/2.30pm	Breast feed or 150–210ml (5–7oz) of formula milk
6pm	Breast feed or 180–240ml (6–8oz) of formula milk
	1–2 tsp baby rice mixed with breast milk, formula or cool, boiled water
10pm	Breast feed or 150–210ml (5–7oz) of formula milk (optional).

Days 7–9

7/7.30am	Breast feed or 180–240ml (6–8 oz) of formula milk
11am	Breast feed or 180–240ml (6–8oz) of formula milk
	1 cube of carrot purée (page 41)

2/2.30pm	Breast feed or 150–210ml (5–7oz) of formula milk
6pm	Breast feed or 180–210ml (6–7oz) of formula milk 1–2 tsp baby rice mixed with breast milk, formula or cool boiled water, plus 1 cube of pear purée
10pm	Breast feed or 150ml (5oz) of formula milk (optional).

Days 10–12

7/7.30am	Breast feed or 180–240ml (6–8 oz) of formula milk
11am	Breast feed or 180–240ml (6–8oz) of formula milk 1 cube of apple purée (page 42)
2/2.30pm	Breast feed or 150–210ml (5–7oz) of formula milk
6pm	Breast feed or 180–210ml (6–7oz) of formula milk 2–3 tsp baby rice mixed with breast milk, formula or cool boiled water
10pm	Breast feed or 150ml (5oz) of formula milk (optional).

Days 13–15

7/7.30am	Breast feed or 180–240ml (6–8 oz) of formula milk
11am	Breast feed or 180–240ml (6–8oz) of formula milk 1 cube of sweet potato purée (page 42)
2/2.30pm	Breast feed or 150–210ml (5–7oz) of formula milk
6pm	Breast feed or 210–240ml (7–8oz) of formula milk 2–3 tsp baby rice mixed with breast milk, formula or cool boiled water plus 1 cube of pear purée
10pm	Breast feed or 100–150ml (3⅓–5oz) of formula milk (optional).

Days 16–18

7/7.30am	Breast feed or 180–240ml (6–8 oz) of formula milk

11am	Breast feed or 180–240ml (6–8oz) of formula milk 1 cube of sweet potato purée or 1–2 tsp baby rice mixed with 1 cube of courgette purée (page 43)
2/2.30pm	Breast feed or 150–210ml (5–7oz) of formula milk
6pm	Breast feed or 210–240ml (7–8oz) of formula milk 3–4 tsp baby rice mixed with breast milk, formula or cool boiled water, plus 1 cube of apple or pear purée
10pm	Breast feed or 100–120ml (3⅓–4oz) of formula milk (optional).

Days 19–21

7am	Breast feed or 180–240ml (6–8 oz) of formula milk
11am	Breast feed or 180–240ml (6–8oz) of formula milk 1–2 cubes of sweet potato purée or 1–2 tsp baby rice mixed with 1 cube of carrot purée
2/2.30pm	Breast feed or 150–210ml (5–7oz) of formula milk
6pm	Breast feed or 210–240ml (7–8oz) of formula milk 3–4 tsp baby rice mixed with breast milk, formula or cool boiled water, plus 1 cube of apple or pear purée
10pm	Breast feed or 60–90ml (2–3oz) of formula milk (optional).

Days 22–24

7am	Breast feed or 180–240ml (6–8 oz) of formula milk
11am	Breast feed or 180–240ml (6–8oz) of formula milk 2 cubes of sweet potato purée or 1–2 tsp baby rice mixed with 1 cube of swede purée (page 43)
2/2.30pm	Breast feed or 150–210ml (5–7oz) of formula milk
6pm	Breast feed or 180–240ml (6–8oz) of formula milk

4–5 tsp baby rice mixed with breast milk, formula or cool boiled water, plus 1 cube of apple or pear purée

10pm   Breast feed or 60–90ml (2–3oz) of formula milk (optional).

Days 25–27

7am   Breast feed or 180–240ml (6–8 oz) of formula milk

11am   Breast feed or 180–240ml (6–8oz) of formula milk
2 cubes of sweet potato purée or 2 tsp baby rice mixed with 1 cube of green bean purée (page 44)

2/2.30pm   Breast feed or 150–210ml (5–7oz) of formula milk

6pm   Breast feed or 180–240ml (6–8oz) of formula milk
4 tsp baby rice mixed with breast milk, formula or cool boiled water, plus 2 cubes of apple purée

10pm   Breast feed or 60ml (2oz) of formula milk (optional).

Days 28–30

7am   Breast feed or 180–240ml (6–8 oz) of formula milk

11am   Breast feed or 180–240ml (6–8oz) of formula milk
2 cubes of carrot purée or 2 tsp baby rice mixed with 1 cube of swede purée

2/2.30pm   Breast feed or 150–210ml (5–7oz) of formula milk

6pm   Breast feed or 180–240ml (6–8oz) of formula milk
4–5 tsp baby rice mixed with breast milk, formula or cool boiled water, plus 2 cubes of apple or pear purée

10pm   Breast feed or 60ml (2oz) of formula milk (optional).
Note: By now your baby should be ready to drop this feed.

Ben: aged four months

Ben weighed just over 3kg (7lb) at birth and was exclusively breast fed for the first two months of his life. Because his weight gain was very low – usually 90–125 g (3–4oz) each week – his mother decided to introduce top-up feeds of formula after each breast feed. Her milk supply diminished even further and by the time he was three months old, Ben was being totally formula fed. By the time he reached 16 weeks Ben was taking five formula feeds a day. He would drink no more than 120–150ml (4–5oz) a feed and even then he would fuss and fret after the first couple of ounces. His weight gain continued to be very low and his mother was advised to introduce baby rice twice a day. At four months of age his mother contacted me because Ben had become very constipated and his daily milk intake had dropped even lower. Ben's elder sister had also been a very poor feeder and his mother was concerned that the same thing was happening with Ben.

My personal opinion was that Ben was not ready to be weaned on to solids. He weighed just over 5kg (11lb) and had never taken more than 150ml (5oz) at any one feed. I felt that introducing baby rice too early had also contributed to Ben's lack of appetite for his milk. At his age and weight, milk would supply him with the right balance of vitamins and minerals, whereas baby rice is really just a filler. I advised Ben's mother to cut out the baby rice altogether for a couple of weeks and introduce more milk feeds, even if it meant going back to feeding Ben in the night.

We put Ben on the six- to eight-week milk feeding schedule, which meant he was getting around seven milk feeds a day: 7am; 10.30/10.45am; 12 noon (top-up feed); 2/2.30pm; 5–6.15pm (split-feed: where the baby has a full feed spread over a longer period) and 10/10.30pm. We continued with this for two weeks, during which time Ben gained nearly 1kg (2lb) in weight and he started to increase

the amount he was taking at individual feeds. The constipation also disappeared and by the end of the third week
Ben was happily taking 210–240ml (7–8oz) at each feed
during the day with a small feed of 150ml (5oz) at 10pm.

Ben was nearly five months old when we re-introduced
baby rice. He continued to enjoy good milk feeds and happily take his solids. Ben's story is typical of a small baby being
weaned too early, with solids being introduced to the detri-
ment of the milk. By introducing a top-up feed and a split-feed,
this increased Ben's overall daily milk intake which resulted
in him gaining weight to the required level. Solids should
never be introduced until a baby weighs nearer 6kg (14lb)
in weight and is taking at least four full breast feeds or four
formula feeds of 210–240ml (7–8oz) a day.

Five to six months

Babies who started weaning at the age of four months should have
tasted baby rice, plus a variety of different vegetables and fruit.
Most will by now be happy to take a combination of two or three
different vegetables at lunch-time. It is important to keep introducing a variety of different vegetables and fruits at this stage.
Research into weaning shows that babies who are introduced to a
wide variety of non-allergy-forming foods from the age of four
months accept a wider range of foods at one year than those
weaned on a restricted diet. Dairy products, wheat, eggs, nuts and
citrus fruits should still be avoided, as they are the foods most likely
to trigger allergies.

Meat, chicken or fish should only be introduced on the advice
of your health visitor. I personally always wait until six months, by
which time the baby is used to digesting a reasonable amount of
solids. I have encountered many feeding problems when protein
has been introduced too early: constipation and serious reduction
in milk intake are two of the main ones. The majority of leading
nutritionists believe that protein can put a strain on the young

baby's kidneys and digestive tract and also recommend waiting until six months. The exception to this would be a very large baby who might need to start weaning slightly sooner in order to receive the necessary protein that his body would require. Take advice from your health visitor if this is the case.

Somewhere between the age of five and six months your baby will probably show signs of hunger long before his 11am feed is due. This is a sign that he is ready to start having breakfast, and a small amount of breakfast cereal can be introduced after his 7am milk feed. Until he reaches the age of six months it is important to choose a cereal that is wheat- and gluten-free.

Daily requirements

By six months most babies are well established on two solid meals a day and heading towards a third.

If your baby is not showing much interest in solids but is drinking a lot of milk, it would be wise to cut back his lunchtime feed to encourage his interest in solids. Some babies get really hooked on milk. They can come to hate the feel of a spoon in their mouth and start to refuse solid food altogether. But remember, your baby still needs a minimum of 600ml (20oz) of breast milk or formula milk a day.

The following guidelines should help to get the balance of solids right, so that he neither reduces his milk too quickly, nor drinks excessive quantities of milk, taking away his appetite for solids.

Weaning guidelines

- If your baby reaches six months, weighs over 7kg (16lb) and shows no signs of wanting breakfast, it would be wise to reduce his milk feed very slightly and offer a small amount of solids.

- Once breakfast is introduced he should be happy to go longer between his feeds. As the amount he eats at breakfast increases, gradually keep pushing the 11am feed later, until he is eating lunch between 11.45am and 12 noon.

• When breakfast has been established for a couple of weeks, you can start to give your baby two-thirds of his milk feed first, then the cereal, finishing with the remainder of the milk. This is known as the 'tier method of feeding'.

• Once he is taking 2–3 cubes of vegetable purée you can start to use the tier method of feeding at lunchtime, alternating between his milk and the solids.

• Food will still need to be puréed, but not so smoothly. This will help prepare your baby for mashed food at six months.

• When barley cereal is introduced, a little chicken stock (page 46) can be used to mix along with the vegetables.

• Once the tier method of eating is introduced at lunchtime (see above) the solids should start to overtake the milk. Keep increasing the solids and gradually reduce the milk feed, preparing your baby to drop this once protein is introduced at six months.

Feeding plan at five to six months

The following feeding plan is intended to be used as a guide, so don't feel anxious if your baby seems to want a little more or less than the recommended serving.

Foods to introduce
Oats, parsnips, mango, peaches, broccoli, avocados, barley, peas and cauliflower.

Days 1–3

7am   Breast feed or 210–240ml (7–8 oz) of formula milk
            1 tsp of pure organic gluten-free cereal mixed with
            breast milk or formula milk

11am	Breast feed or 150–210ml (5–7oz) of formula milk
	4 cubes of sweet potato, carrot or courgette purée mashed together
2/2.30pm	Breast feed or 150–210ml (5–7oz) of formula milk
6pm	Breast feed or 210–240ml (7–8oz) of formula milk
	4 tsp of baby rice mixed with breast milk, formula milk or cool boiled water, plus 2 cubes of apple purée.

Days 4–6

7am	Breast feed or 210–240ml (7–8 oz) of formula milk
	1 tsp of oat cereal mixed with expressed or formula milk plus 1 cube of peach purée (page 44)
11am	Breast feed or 150–180ml (5–6oz) of formula milk
	4–5 cubes of sweet potato, swede and green bean purée mashed together
2/2.30pm	Breast feed or 150–180ml (5–6oz) of formula milk
6pm	Breast feed or 210–240ml (7–8oz) of formula milk
	4 tsp of baby rice mixed with breast milk, formula milk or cool boiled water, plus 2 cubes of apple or pear purée.

Days 7–9

7am	Breast feed or 210–240ml (7–8 oz) of formula milk
	1 tsp of oat cereal mixed with breast milk or formula, plus 1 cube of apple or peach purée
11am	Breast feed or 150–180ml (5–6oz) of formula milk
	2 tbsp of mashed avocado mixed with 2 cubes of apple purée
2/2.30pm	Breast feed or 150–180ml (5–6oz) of formula milk
6pm	Breast feed or 210–240ml (7–8oz) of formula milk
	4–5 tsp of baby rice mixed with expressed milk or formula, plus 2 cubes of apple, pear or peach purée.

Days 10–12

7am   Breast feed or 210–240ml (7–8 oz) of formula milk
              2 tsp of oat cereal mixed with expressed milk or
              formula, plus 1 cube of apple, pear or peach purée

11am   Breast feed or 120–150ml (4–5oz) of formula milk
              3 cubes of sweet potato purée mixed with 2 cubes of
              courgette or carrot purée

2/2.30pm   Breast feed or 150–180ml (5–6oz) of formula milk

6pm   Breast feed or 210–240ml (7–8oz) of formula milk
              4–5 tsp of baby rice mixed with expressed milk or
              formula, plus 2 cubes of apple, pear or peach purée.

Days 13–15

7am   Breast feed or 210–240ml (7–8 oz) of formula milk
              2 tsp of oat cereal mixed with expressed milk or
              formula, plus 1 cube of peach purée

11am   Breast feed or 120–150ml (4–5oz) of formula milk
              2 cubes of sweet potato purée mixed with 1 cube of
              carrot purée and 1 cube of courgette purée

2/2.30pm   Breast feed or 150–180ml (5–6oz) of formula milk

6pm   Breast feed or 210–240ml (7–8oz) of formula milk
              5–6 tsp of baby rice mixed with expressed milk or
              formula, plus 2 cubes of apple, pear or peach purée.

Days 16–18

7am   Breast feed or 210–240ml (7–8 oz) of formula milk
              2 tsp of oat cereal mixed with expressed milk or
              formula, plus 2 cubes of apple, pear or peach purée

11.30am   Breast feed or 90–120ml (3–4oz) of formula milk
              2 cubes of swede purée, mixed with 2 cubes of
              carrot purée and 1 tbsp of pure organic baby barley
              cereal mixed with 1 tbsp of home-made chicken

stock (page 46)

2/2.30pm	Breast feed or 150–180ml (5–6oz) of formula milk
6pm	Breast feed or 210–240ml (7–8oz) of formula milk 4–5 tsp of baby rice mixed with expressed milk, formula milk or cool boiled water, plus 2 cubes of apple, pear or peach purée.

Days 19–21

7/7.30am	Breast feed or 210–240ml (7–8 oz) of formula milk 3 tsp of oat cereal mixed with expressed milk or formula, plus 2 cubes of apple, pear or peach purée
11.45am	Breast feed or 90ml (3oz) of formula milk 3 cubes of sweet potato purée, mixed with 2 cubes of cauliflower purée (page 45)
2/2.30pm	Breast feed or 150–180ml (5–6oz) of formula milk
6pm	Breast feed or 210–240ml (7–8oz) of formula milk 5–6 tsp of baby rice mixed with expressed milk, formula milk or cool boiled water, plus 2 cubes of apple, pear or peach purée.

Days 22–24

7/7.30am	Breast feed or 210–240ml (7–8 oz) of formula milk 3 tsp of oat cereal mixed with expressed milk or formula, plus 2 cubes of apple, pear or peach purée
11.30am	Breast feed or 90–120ml (3–4oz) of formula milk 3 cubes of sweet potato purée, mixed with 2 cubes of broccoli purée (page 45)
2/2.30pm	Breast feed or 150–180ml (5–6oz) of formula milk
6pm	Breast feed or 210–240ml (7–8oz) of formula milk 5–6 tsp of baby rice mixed with expressed milk, formula milk or cool boiled water, plus 2 cubes of apple, pear or peach or purée.

Days 25–27

7/7.30am   Breast feed or 210–240ml (7–8 oz) of formula milk
3 tsp of oat cereal mixed with expressed milk or
formula mixed with half a mashed banana

11.30am   Breast feed or 90–120ml (3–4oz) of formula milk
3 cubes of sweet potato purée, mixed with 2 cubes
of carrot purée, plus 1 cube of cauliflower purée

2/2.30pm   Breast feed or 150–180ml (5–6oz) of formula milk

6pm   Breast feed or 210–240ml (7–8oz) of formula milk
5–6 tsp of baby rice mixed with expressed milk,
formula milk or cool boiled water, plus 2 cubes of
apple, pear or peach purée.

Days 28–30

7/7.30am   Breast feed or 210–240ml (7–8 oz) of formula milk
4 tsp of oat cereal mixed with expressed milk or
formula, plus 2 cubes of apple, pear or peach purée

11.30am   Breast feed or 90–120ml (3–4oz) of formula milk
2 cubes of sweet potato purée mixed with 2 cubes of
parsnip purée, plus 2 cubes of broccoli purée

2/2.30pm   Breast feed or 150–180ml (5–6oz) of formula milk

6pm   Breast feed or 210–240ml (7–8oz) of formula milk
5–6 tsp of baby rice mixed with expressed milk or
formula, plus 2 cubes of pear purée.

Hannah: aged 5½ months

Hannah was introduced to a variety of different fruit and vegetables between four and five months. At five months she went to stay with her grandparents for four days while her parents were on a business trip. During that time she suddenly started to get very fussy with her solids, eventually refusing the home-made vegetable purées. Her grandparents – anxious that she would go hungry – started giving her fruit purée at every meal. By the time her parents returned from their trip, Hannah would scream every time she was offered anything other than baby rice and fruit purée.

Feeding soon became a battle of wills as Hannah's mother tried to coax and cajole her into eating vegetables. She tried disguising the vegetables by mixing them with lots of fruit but Hannah still refused. After two weeks of battling and screaming at every meal she rang me for advice. As Hannah was under six months old, I advised her mother to take her right back to the very first stage of weaning. For three days, Hannah should be given baby rice mixed with milk and without fruit. On the fourth day I suggested that half a teaspoonful of puréed courgette should be mixed in with five teaspoonfuls of baby rice mixed with milk. Over the next few days Hannah's mother was to increase the courgette purée by no more than half a teaspoon each day. Once Hannah was taking two teaspoons of courgette purée with rice, I suggested that we try replacing the rice at lunchtime with sweet potato mixed with milk and courgette. Hannah happily took the sweet potato and the following day we introduced half a teaspoon of carrot with the sweet potato. Over the next couple of weeks we very slowly introduced different vegetables along with the sweet potato or baby rice, always starting off with no more than half a teaspoon, and always increasing it very slowly.

By the time Hannah was six-and-a-half months old she was happily eating a variety of different vegetables at lunch and tea, plus chicken and lentil casserole. We did introduce fruit again but kept it to breakfast time until Hannah was seven months old. Obviously fruit plays an important part in a baby's diet but if your baby shows signs of developing a very sweet tooth, I would suggest that you restrict the amount you introduce until your baby is well established on vegetables.

When trying to solve a problem like Hannah's it is very important to take things very slowly and not increase the ratio of vegetables to baby rice too quickly. The recommended age for starting to wean is four to six months, and until a baby reaches six months milk still supplies the right balance of nutrients. With some babies I have found it necessary to re-introduce a small feed at 10pm for a week or so until the quantity of solids is increased back to what the baby was eating previously.

Your questions answered

Q Why do you advise introducing solids at the 11am feed? Many of my friends who have weaned their babies started doing so after the first feed in the morning or after the 2/2.30pm feed.

A • I always start solids at the 11am feed as it is easier to push the 11am feed to a proper lunch at 12 noon than to try to bring the solids forwards from 2/2.30pm to noon. Also, up until the age of six months, milk is still the most important source of food for your baby, providing him with the right balance of vitamins and minerals. By giving your baby his first solids after the 11am feed you can be reassured that he has had nearly half of his daily intake before noon.

- If you start solids at 2/2.30pm it could put him off the 6pm feed and make him cut back too much on it. If he does cut back on the 6pm feed, he may wake earlier for his 10pm feed, which could have a knock-on effect on the time he wakes in the morning.

- If you give solids after the first feed in the morning it is very possible that your baby will cut back too quickly on the amount of milk he drinks at the 11am feed. If his 11am feed is reduced, it could also affect his lunchtime nap as he may wake up earlier due to hunger. This could result in him taking too big a feed at 2/2.30pm, and cutting back at the 6pm feed, which could affect his night-time sleep.

- Starting solids at the 11am feed will also make it easier to establish three solid meals a day. The majority of babies wake between 6am and 7am, and when breakfast is introduced it usually comes between 7am and 8am. As their need for solids increases it becomes very difficult to get them to wait until 2/2.30pm for their next lot of solids. This can result in two problems: the baby's need for the 11am milk feed increases, instead of decreasing, which can result in his taking less milk or solids at 2/2.30pm, and getting hungry long before his next feed. Alternatively, if you decide to bring the 2/2.30pm feed forward it means the baby's lunchtime nap will be cut short. Either way you could end up with a baby who is very grumpy all afternoon because he is too tired or too hungry.

- If a very hungry baby has had no reaction to the baby rice within three days, I would transfer the rice to after the 6pm feed.

Q My baby of four-and-a-half months gets very tired by
6.15pm. He will take his full milk feed but is too irritable
to take the baby rice, and he has now started waking up at
9.00pm looking for a big milk feed. He has also started to
cut back on his morning feed since his late feed has
increased.
I have tried moving the rice to 5pm, but he then cuts back
on his 6.15pm feed, and again needs to feed at 9.00pm,
with the same result – he cuts back on his morning feed.

A • I would try giving him two-thirds of his milk feed at
5.30–5.45pm followed by his baby rice, and wait until
6.30pm before starting his bath. Although he will be getting tired, the bath should revive him just enough to take
the remainder of his milk feed at around 6.50pm.

• As he gets a little older he should begin to get less tired at
6.15pm. When this happens, try giving him half of his
baby rice at 5pm, a bath at 6pm, then his full milk feed,
followed by the remainder of the baby rice.

• By the time he gets to six months you should be able to
transfer all of his solids to 5pm, and give him a full milk
feed after his bath. However, should you find he begins
to wake earlier in the morning it may be advisable to go
back to splitting the solid feed for a further two or three
weeks.

Q Which is the best food to introduce first?

A • The reason we wean babies is because milk alone no
longer satisfies their hunger, and in my experience, baby
rice does this best. Baby rice is also very bland and makes
the transition from milk to solids easier. If baby rice is
tolerated I would then introduce some pear purée (page

41) and if the baby had no reaction, I would always mix a small amount of pear with the baby rice. This will help prevent him from becoming constipated, which can happen to some babies when solids are first introduced.

- Once these two foods are established, it is best to concentrate on introducing a variety of vegetables as described on page 17. Research has shown that babies weaned on fruit are less likely to thrive than those weaned on baby rice. Most experts advise that all babies should start weaning on baby rice (page 15).

- I also believe that it is very important to wean babies on home-made food as opposed to jars of fruit and vegetables. The taste of commercial baby food, no matter how pure, is always different from that of food cooked at home. I have also found that babies who are weaned on fresh home-made food are much less likely to become fussy eaters.

Q How will I know how much solid food to give my baby?

A
- For the first six months, milk is still the most important part of your baby's diet, and he will need a minimum of 600ml (20oz) a day. During the first month if you always offer the milk first, then the solids, you can be sure he will take exactly the amount of solids he needs. This will prevent him from replacing his milk too quickly with solids.

- Between four and five months most babies should ideally be having four full milk feeds between 7am and 7pm, and some may still need a small milk feed at 10pm. (A full feed is defined as a formula feed of 240ml/8oz or a breast feed.) As your baby increases his solids during the day he should start to reduce the amounts he takes at 10pm, and most babies will cut this feed out by five months of age.

- Although all babies' appetites are different, I find that, on average, a baby who starts off taking about one teaspoonful of baby rice mixed with milk at the 6pm feed will have gradually increased this amount to three to four teaspoonfuls mixed with milk and two cubes of pear purée (page 41) by the time he has reached five months. At lunchtime most babies will have worked their way from a cube of vegetable purée to three to four cubes. Very small babies may be taking less than this and very large babies may need slightly more. Be guided by your baby.

- The most important thing to remember during this first month of weaning is that any solid food you give your baby should be in addition to the milk, not as a replacement for it. A baby who is taking a lot more than the quantities I have recommended and cuts right back on his milk will be losing valuable nutrients. Remember, solids at this stage are really first tastes and fillers, not meals.

Q **When should I start to reduce the amount of milk my baby drinks?**

A
- Up to the age of six months your baby still needs a minimum of 600ml (20oz) of milk a day. From five months more milk will be used to mix his baby rice, cereal and solids, so although the actual amount he drinks reduces slightly, his daily intake should remain the same.

- When breakfast is introduced between five and six months he may drink slightly less, but the amount is usually made up by that used on his breakfast cereal.

- Between five and six months the tier method of eating (page 25) should be established at lunchtime; give him half the milk feed first, then some solids, followed by more milk. This will encourage your baby to cut back slightly on his milk feed and increase his solids, preparing him for a feeding pattern of three meals a day at six months.

- With breast-fed babies a feed from one breast can be classed as half a milk feed.

Q **When should I introduce my baby to breakfast cereal, and what type of breakfast cereal should I use?**

A
- Once your baby shows signs of being hungry long before his 11am feed, he is probably ready to be given a small amount of breakfast cereal. This usually happens between the fifth and sixth month.

- All cereal should be wheat- and gluten-free until the age of six months. I find that organic oatmeal cereal with a small amount of puréed fruit is a favourite with most babies.

- Continue to give your baby most of his milk first. Increasing his breakfast cereal could make him cut back too quickly on his lunchtime solids and milk. If this happens it could affect his lunchtime sleep as he might wake up earlier because he is hungry.

- After a couple of weeks you should give your baby about two-thirds of his milk first, then the cereal, finishing up with the remainder of the milk. If you find he frequently refuses the remainder of his milk after the cereal then you should return to giving him most of his milk first.

Q **My baby is five months old, weighs nearly 8kg (18lb), has always fed on demand and is still waking twice in the night for a feed, at around midnight (he doesn't feed for long at this time), then again at 4am. I thought that when solids were introduced he would sleep longer in the night.**

I have been trying unsuccessfully to introduce solids since four months, but he simply refuses to even open his mouth when he sees the spoon. I have tried not feeding him in the night but he just screams and screams until he is fed. He does seem to be genuinely hungry.

A • I am sure that a great many babies who are fed on demand do put themselves into a routine, but judging from the number of phone calls I receive each month a huge number do not. Sadly for these babies, a failure to structure milk feeding in the early days can lead to them becoming 'milkoholics', which can lead to the steadfast refusal of solids. I am sure that your baby is genuinely hungry in the night. However, as long as he continues to be on six milk feeds a day he will be unlikely to accept solids.

• To solve this problem you need gradually to reduce the amount of milk he is taking in the night. However, as you have already discovered, leaving him to yell in the night does not solve the problem, as he really *is* hungry. In my experience this problem is easier to solve, and less stressful, if you start off by reducing his milk intake during the day to encourage his interest in solids.

• I suggest that for several days you cut out the 2/2.30pm feed in the afternoon, as it is easier to deal with a fretful baby during the day than at night. By 4.30/5pm he should be getting very hungry and this is when you should try giving him 1 teaspoonful of baby rice mixed with breast milk or formula. Try to get him to take at least half of the solids, but do not push him so much that he gets very upset. As long as he takes a small amount he can then be given the first breast. The second breast should be given as usual after the bath. Because he will have taken slightly less than normal at the 6pm feed he should feed better at the 10pm feed, which should help him to go longer in the night. After a few days of cutting out the 2/2.30pm milk feed there should be an improvement in the amount of solids he is taking at 4.30/5pm. Once this happens he should automatically start to take less milk in the night, which should continue to have a knock-on effect on the amount he is eating in the day. As his daytime appetite increases, solids can be introduced at the 11am feed.

- Normally I would advise that a baby of this age always be given the milk feed first, but as your baby is clearly drinking more milk than he needs over a 24-hour period, I would advise that you give him only one breast at 11am, then offer the solids before giving him the second breast.

- When he is down to feeding once in the night (between 7pm and 7am) a small 2.30pm milk feed can be re-introduced. The evening solids can then be moved to later. He should be given the first breast at 5.30pm, followed by the baby rice, then the second breast at 6.45pm after the bath. The bath time would also have to be changed to 6.30pm.

- Once he is taking two to three cubes of vegetable purée at lunchtime, and two to three teaspoons of baby rice in the evening, in addition to four good milk feeds during the day, he should not need to feed between 11pm and 7am. He may still wake up through habit, however. If this is the case I would suggest you try offering him cool boiled water in the night. If he takes a couple of ounces and still won't settle he can be offered a small breast feed. This way he will still be taking less than if he were getting a full breast feed.

- Once he has increased his solids to four cubes of vegetable purée at 11am and four teaspoons of baby rice and two cubes of fruit purée in the evening, introduce some cereal at breakfast. Once he is taking this amount of solids, in addition to his milk, he will not need to be fed in the middle of the night. If he continues to wake it is certainly due to habit and not hunger and you may have to consider sleep training.

Q **Do I need to sterilise my baby's feeding bowls and spoons and the utensils I use for cooking his food?**

A • Once he reaches six months there is no need to sterilise your baby's dishes and spoons. They can be put in the dishwasher, or washed thoroughly in hot soapy water, then rinsed and left to air dry.

• Between four and six months, the pots, cooking utensils and ice cube trays used for preparing weaning food can either be put in the dishwasher or washed in hot soapy water, rinsed and then have boiled water poured over them before being left to air dry.

• Bottles should be sterilised until your baby is one year old.

Q **Which foods are most likely to cause allergies and what are the symptoms?**

A • The most common allergy-causing foods are cow's milk products, wheat, fish, eggs, citrus fruits and nuts. Some experts believe that in families with a history of allergies, introducing these foods should be delayed until nearer eight months – particularly wheat and dairy products, which are the two foods that seem to be the main cause of most allergies. If there is a history of allergies in your family it would be wise to discuss this with your health visitor before introducing the above foods.

• Symptoms of allergies include rashes, wheezing,

coughing, running nose, sore bottom, diarrhoea, irritability and swelling of the eyes.

• Keeping a detailed diary when you are weaning can be a big help when you are trying to establish the cause of any of the above symptoms.

• Any of the symptoms above can also be caused by house mites, animal fur, wool and certain soap and household cleaning agents. If in doubt, always check with your doctor to rule out any other possible causes or illness.

Recipes for four to six months

Ultra-smooth fruit and vegetable purées make ideal first stage weaning foods, and have the added advantage that they can be made in advance in batches, then frozen and defrosted when necessary. Freeze the purées in sections of an ice cube tray, then, as weaning progresses, you can increase the amount from one to two, three or more cubes per meal. Once weaning is well under way, different-flavoured cubes can be combined.

All the recipes described in the following pages can be frozen. If you choose, you can substitute steaming for boiling, but always ensure vegetables are tender. See pages 13–14 for general advice on freezing and defrosting.

GENERAL TIPS

• About 8 weeks after weaning has begun you can begin to introduce your baby to uncooked fruit purée.

• If your blender or food processor purées the skin finely, you can stop sieving foods from 6 months and as weaning gets well under way, begin to make purées slightly coarser by mashing ripe fruit with a fork.

• The riper the fruit, the more naturally sweet it is.

Pear purée

Makes about 20 cubes

- 1kg (2lb 4oz) **dessert pears**

1. Wash the pears under cold running water, cut into quarters, remove core and any pith. Peel and put in a saucepan and cover with freshly boiled, filtered water. Bring to the boil, cover, then lower the heat and simmer for 5–7 minutes or until tender. Remove from the cooking liquid and purée to a smooth texture in a blender or food processor, using some of the cooking liquid to get the right consistency. Allow the mixture to cool.

2. Spoon the mixture into ice cube trays and put in the freezer. Leave to open-freeze for 3–4 hours or until fully frozen. Remove the cubes and put into clearly labelled freezer bags. Return to the freezer and use when necessary, defrosting thoroughly before use.

Carrot purée

Makes about 25 cubes

- 1kg (2lb 4oz) **carrots**

1. Wash the carrots under cold running water. Top and tail and either scrub well or peel. Put them in a saucepan and cover with freshly boiled filtered water. Bring to the boil, cover, then lower the heat and simmer for 12–14 minutes or until tender. Remove from the cooking liquid and purée in a blender or food processor, using some of the cooking liquid to get the right consistency. Allow the mixture to cool.

2. Spoon the mixture into ice cube trays and freeze as for pear purée (above).

Apple purée

Makes about 25 cubes

- 1kg (2lb 4oz) **eating apples**

1. Wash the apples under cold running water; quarter, peel and
   core them. Put all the prepared apples into a saucepan and
   cover with freshly boiled, filtered water. Bring to the boil,
   cover, then lower the heat and simmer for 5–7 minutes or
   until tender. Remove from the cooking liquid and purée to a
   smooth texture in a blender or food processor, using some of
   the cooking liquid to get the right consistency. Allow the mixture to cool.
2. Spoon the mixture into ice cube trays and freeze as for pear
   purée (page 41).

Sweet potato purée

Makes about 22 cubes

- 750g (1lb 8oz) **sweet potatoes**

1. Wash the sweet potatoes under cold running water, then peel.
   Put them in a saucepan and cover with freshly boiled, filtered
   water. Bring to the boil, cover, then lower the heat and
   simmer for 15 minutes or until tender. Remove from the cooking liquid. Mash the flesh with a fork, and press through a
   sieve. Allow the mixture to cool.
2. Spoon the mixture into ice cube trays and freeze as for pear
   purée (page 41).

Note: Ordinary potatoes can be substituted for sweet potatoes if
preferred.

Courgette purée

Makes about 12 cubes

- 450g (1lb) **courgettes**

1. Wash the courgettes under cold running water. Cut off the ends and slice the courgettes. Put them in a saucepan and cover with freshly boiled, filtered water. Bring to the boil, uncovered, then lower the heat. Simmer uncovered for about 5–7 minutes or until tender. Remove from cooking liquid and purée in a blender or food processor to a smooth texture, using some of the cooking liquid to get the right consistency. Allow the mixture to cool.

2. Spoon the mixture into ice cube trays and freeze as for pear purée (page 41).

Swede purée

Makes about 16 cubes

- 1 small **swede**, weighing about 350 g (12 oz)

1. Wash the swede under cold running water. Peel and slice then dice into even-sized cubes. Put in a saucepan and cover with plenty of freshly boiled, filtered water. Bring to the boil, cover, then lower the heat and simmer for 10–12 minutes or until tender. Remove the swede from the pan and purée to a smooth texture in a blender or food processor, adding some of the cooking liquid to get the right consistency. Allow the mixture to cool.

2. Spoon the mixture into ice cube trays and freeze as for pear purée (page 41).

Green bean purée
Makes about 12 cubes

- 225 g (8 oz) **green beans**

1. Top and tail the green beans and remove the strings. Wash the beans in a colander under cold running water. Put them in a saucepan and cover with freshly boiled, filtered water. Bring to the boil, then lower the heat and simmer, uncovered, for 4–5 minutes or until tender. Remove from the pan and purée to a smooth texture in a blender or food processor, using some of the cooking liquid to get the right consistency. Allow the mixture to cool.
2. Spoon the mixture into ice cube trays and freeze as for pear purée (page 41).

Peach purée
Makes about 20 cubes

- 3 fresh ripe **peaches**
- 4 tbsp boiled filtered **water**

1. Wash the peaches under cold running water. Peel, halve and stone them and roughly chop the flesh. Put the flesh into a saucepan with the water. Bring to the boil, then cover, lower the heat and simmer for 10 minutes or until tender.
2. Remove from the cooking liquid and purée to a smooth texture in a blender or food processor.
3. Spoon the mixture into ice cube trays and freeze as for pear purée (page 41).

Note: Scale the amounts down to just 1 ripe peach (or nectarine) and 1 tbsp boiling water if not planning to freeze the recipe.

Cauliflower purée

Makes about 30 cubes

- 1kg (2lb 4oz) **cauliflower**, cut into small florets

1. Wash the cauliflower florets under cold running water. Put into a saucepan and cover with freshly boiled, filtered water. Bring to the boil, then lower the heat and simmer, uncovered, for 8–10 minutes or until tender. Purée to a smooth texture in a blender or food processor, adding some of the cooking liquid to get the right consistency.
2. Spoon the mixture into ice cube trays and freeze as for pear purée (page 41).

Broccoli purée

Makes about 20 cubes

- 450g (1lb) **broccoli**, cut into small florets

1. Wash the broccoli florets under cold running water. Put into a saucepan of freshly boiled, filtered water. Bring to the boil, cover, then lower the heat and simmer for 4–6 minutes or until tender (test stalks). Remove from the cooking liquid and purée to a smooth texture in a blender, or food processor, adding some of the cooking liquid to get the right consistency. Allow the mixture to cool.
2. Spoon the mixture into ice cube trays and freeze as for pear purée (page 41).

Basic stocks

Home-made chicken stock
Makes 1 litre (1¾ pints)

- 1 **chicken carcass**
- 1 **onion**, peeled and quartered
- 1 **carrot**, peeled and diced
- 1 stick **celery** or half a **leek** (green top) (optional) sliced
- 1 **bay leaf** (optional)
- 2 litres (3½ pints) cold filtered **water**

1. Put all the ingredients into a large saucepan, bring to the boil then lower the heat, half-cover with a lid and simmer for 2 hours or until the liquid has reduced by half.
2. Strain the stock into a jug, cover and leave to cool. Store in the fridge and use within 24 hours, or freeze in small containers.

Home-made vegetable stock
Makes 1 litre (1¾ pints)

- 1 **onion**, peeled and quartered
- 2 **carrots**, peeled and diced
- 3 sticks **celery**, trimmed and sliced
- ½ **leek** (green top), sliced
- 1.5 litre (2½ pints) cold filtered **water**

1. Put all the ingredients into a saucepan, bring to the boil, then lower the heat, half-cover with a lid and simmer for 1 hour.
2. Strain the stock into a jug, discarding the vegetables. Cover and leave to cool. Store in the fridge and use within 24 hours, or freeze in small containers.

3 Second Stage Weaning: six to nine months

During the second stage of weaning, the amount of milk your baby drinks will gradually reduce as his intake of solids increases. It is, however, important that he still receives a minimum of 500–600ml (16–20oz) a day of breast or formula milk. This is usually divided between three milk feeds and milk used in food and cooking, with more milk being used in cooking as sauces are introduced. At this stage of weaning you should be aiming towards establishing three well-balanced meals a day, so that by the time your baby reaches nine months of age, he should be getting most of his nourishment from solids. During this time it is important to keep introducing a wide variety of foods from the different food types (page 17) so that your baby's nutritional needs are met.

This stage of weaning sees the introduction of stronger-tasting foods, such as chicken, fish and more cereals. Care should still be taken when introducing different foods – particularly fish, dairy and wheat products – as they can cause reactions in some allergic babies. Try to introduce these one at a time so that, in the event of a reaction, it will be obvious which food has caused it.

Breakfast
Your baby will probably still be desperate for milk first thing in the morning, so allow him at least two-thirds of his morning milk quota before attempting to offer him solids. Once he is nearer nine

months of age he will most likely show signs of not being hungry for his milk and this is a good time to try offering him his breakfast milk from a beaker. Wheat-based cereals can now be introduced, although you may want to delay this stage if you have a family history of allergies – check with your health visitor, GP or a dietician. All being well, choose organic cereals that are fortified with iron and B vitamins and check the labels to make sure they are both sugar- and salt-free. You can always sweeten them by adding fresh fruit. It need no longer be cooked – simply mash it or grate it on to the breakfast cereal. Try to alternate the cereals between oat- and wheat-based, even if your baby shows a preference for one over the other. In my experience a baby will in the long term take a dislike to even his most favourite cereal if it is offered every day.

Once your baby is finger feeding, and if your baby is still hungry after his cereal, you can offer a selection of fruits and yoghurt, along with lightly buttered toast.

Lunch

If your baby is eating a proper breakfast you will be able to push lunch to somewhere between 11.45am and 12 noon. However, should he be eating only a small amount at breakfast he will need to eat slightly earlier. Likewise, a baby who is having only a very short nap in the morning may also need to have lunch slightly earlier. It is important to remember that an over-tired, over-hungry baby will not feed as well, so take a cue as to the timing of lunch from him.

During this stage of weaning protein should be introduced at lunchtime. Whenever possible, try to buy organic chicken and meat which is free from additives and growth stimulators. I usually find that during the early stages of introducing protein, cooking it as a casserole with root vegetables makes it much more palatable as many babies baulk at the strong flavour of protein which has been cooked on its own then mixed with vegetables.

Pork, bacon and processed hams should not be given as they have a high salt content. You should still continue to cook all food without additional salt or added sugar, although a small amount of fresh herbs can be introduced at around nine months of age. Once your baby is established on protein at lunchtime, his milk feed should be replaced with a drink of cool boiled water or well-diluted juice from a beaker. You might find that he drinks only a small amount from the beaker and may look for an increase of milk in the 2.30pm milk feed, or an increase of cool boiled water later in the day.

If you are introducing your baby to a vegetarian diet, it is important to seek expert advice on getting the balance of amino acids right. Vegetables are incomplete sources of amino acids when cooked separately, and need to be combined correctly to provide your baby with a complete source of protein.

If your baby is still hungry after his main meal, offer a piece of cheese, a breadstick, chopped fruit or yoghurt.

Tea

During the sixth month, the cereal and fruit given at the 6pm feed can be replaced with a proper (vegetarian) tea at 5pm. If you always make sure that your baby has a well-balanced breakfast and lunch you can be more relaxed about this meal. Some babies can get very tired and fractious around this time of the day, so offer foods that are quick and easy to prepare – thick vegetable soups and vegetable bakes that have been prepared and frozen in advance are always a good standby. Pasta, or a baked potato, served with vegetables and sauces is also nutritious and easy. A very hungry baby can also be offered a milk pudding or yoghurt.

Once your baby is finger feeding, a selection of mini sandwiches or rice cakes with vegetable or fruit spreads will usually be popular. If he gets very tired and refuses to eat, try something easy like rice pudding and fruit or a sugar-free yoghurt mixed with fruit.

A small drink of cool boiled water or well-diluted juice can be offered from a beaker with his solids. A good milk feed at bedtime is still important at this stage. If he starts cutting back too much on his milk, check that you are not giving him too much to drink or overfeeding him at teatime.

Daily requirements

During the second stage of weaning it is important to work towards establishing three proper solid meals a day. Iron is a significant nutritional consideration at this time. This important mineral is essential for your baby's mental and physical development and for the formation of red blood cells. All babies are born with a natural store of iron in their bodies, but by the time they reach six months of age most of it will have been used up, so it is very important now to include iron-rich foods, such as red meat, green leafy vegetables, dried fruits and iron-enriched breakfast cereals, in his diet. To help improve absorption of foods rich in iron always try to serve them with vitamin C-containing fruits and vegetables, e.g. citrus fruits, berries or a small beaker of pure fruit juice. Once you have established protein at lunchtime, it is important to drop the lunchtime milk feed – giving milk to drink with protein reduces iron absorption by up to 50 per cent.

Your baby still needs 500–600ml (18–20oz) of breast or formula milk a day, inclusive of milk used for mixing food. If he starts to reject his milk, cut right back on his 2.30pm milk feed to ensure that he takes a good milk feed first thing in the morning and at bedtime. Offer him extra yoghurt and cheese, and include sauces and puddings in his diet to ensure that his daily milk requirements are met.

Weaning guidelines

- Between the ages of six and nine months your baby should have two to three servings of carbohydrates a day. These should be in the form of cereal, wholemeal bread, pasta or potatoes.

- Choose less refined sugar-free cereals such as Weetabix or Ready Brek, which are rich in iron and vitamins. These can be served with fresh mashed or grated fruit.

- Your baby needs at least two servings of vegetables and fruit a day, with, ideally, more vegetables than fruit. Fruit need no longer be cooked or puréed. Start off by offering it grated and mashed, progressing to small pieces of soft bite-sized pieces.

• Your baby will need one serving of animal protein a day, a serving starting at approximately 25g (1oz) and increasing to around 50g (2oz). When serving a vegetarian meal, make sure you follow the guidelines for combining vegetable protein to ensure that your baby receives a complete protein meal. It is always wise to speak to your health visitor or a dietician before giving a wholly vegetarian diet to your baby.

• Remove all fat, skin and bones from meat and poultry and avoid meats such as ham, pork and bacon which are too high in fat and salt. Continue to cook meats with vegetables in casseroles but these can now be pulsed together in the blender instead of being puréed into a totally smooth consistency.

• From six months onwards vegetables can be mashed instead of puréed. Once your baby is happy taking mashed, but not *lumpy*, food you can start to introduce small amounts of finger foods. Vegetables should be cooked until soft then offered in cube-sized pieces or steamed and then mixed to the right consistency with cool filtered water. Once your baby is managing softly cooked pieces of vegetables and soft pieces of raw fruit, you can try him with pieces of toast or a low-sugar rusk. By nine months, if your baby has several teeth, he should be able to manage some chopped raw vegetables. Dried fruit can be given now but it should be washed first and soaked overnight.

• Egg yolks can be introduced, but must be hard-boiled. Tinned fish such as tuna may also be included, but choose fish in vegetable oil, as fish canned in brine has a higher salt content.

• Once your baby is self-feeding it is important to wash his hands thoroughly before and after meals. He should never be left unattended once he is self-feeding because of the risk of choking.

- When protein is well established at lunchtime, the milk feed should be replaced with a drink of water or well-diluted juice – try to encourage him to drink this from a beaker. Once he is happy to do this, introduce a beaker for his 2.30pm feed. By eight months, try to get him to take at least some of his breakfast milk from a beaker.

- By the end of nine months, try to encourage your baby to drink all of his breakfast milk from a beaker. Apart from his bedtime milk feed all other milk feeds and drinks should ideally be given from a beaker.

- At mealtimes, it is best to serve water or well-diluted pure juice after your baby has eaten most of his solids; that way the edge will not be taken off his appetite.

- Olive oil can be introduced in cooking at six months and small quantities of herbs used in cooking from eight months.

- A very hungry baby who is taking three full milk feeds a day, plus three good solid meals, may need a small drink and a piece of fruit mid-morning.

- Small amounts of unsalted butter and full-fat cow's milk (preferably organic) can be used in cooking, but cow's milk should not be given as a drink yet as it is too low in iron.

- By the end of six months your baby will probably be ready to sit in a high chair for his meals. Always ensure that he is properly strapped in and never left unattended. Between eight and nine months he may show signs of wanting to use his spoon. To encourage this, use two spoons. Load one for him to try and get the food into his mouth and use the other to actually get the food in. You can help his co-ordination by holding his wrist and gently guiding his spoon into his mouth.

Feeding plan at six to nine months

When your baby reaches six months you can introduce chicken, fish, meat, pulses and dairy products. I would advise that you introduce these foods slowly during the early stages, introducing a new food every three days to ensure that your baby does not have a bad response to a particular food. Start by replacing two of his vegetable cubes with two cubes of the more simple chicken, fish, meat or pulse recipes. Increase the amount by one or two cubes a day until your baby's meal consists totally of one of the protein recipes.

It is very easy to get into the habit of serving the same favourite foods to your baby, but this could lead to him becoming very fussy about the foods he eats. I therefore advise that once your baby is established on the different protein meals, you should use the feeding plans as a guide to ensure that your baby receives a variety of different foods and meals each week.

Once a protein is established at lunchtime, the rice and fruit in the evening can gradually be replaced with other savoury foods. By the time your baby reaches seven months, his daily feeding plan should look similar to the feeding plans that follow. Parents and carers should use these plans as a guide. All babies differ, so don't feel anxious if your child doesn't appear to like a particular food or seems to want a little more or less. Be guided by your baby.

This plan covers a two-week period, so for the weeks following continue to offer your baby a variation of the menus mentioned.

Foods to introduce

Wheat-based baby cereals, pasta, raw fruits such as raw fresh apricots and soaked, cooked dried apricots, melon, cooked plums and a greater variety of vegetables, including coloured peppers, pumpkin, cabbage and later spinach, Brussels sprouts and celery. Tomatoes and well-diluted unsweetened fruit juices can be introduced if there is no history of allergy.

Meat and fish may be introduced – use mild-tasting chicken, cod or haddock (not smoked) to begin with, then move on to lamb at seven to eight months, along with red lentils and butter beans. Yoghurt, mild Cheddar cheese, small amounts of unsalted butter and cow's milk in cooking can be included as well as first finger foods such as cooked toast fingers, cooked carrot or broccoli sticks.

Note: If your baby has no reaction to any new foods you have introduced at this stage the following feeding plan can be used as a guide to ensure your baby eats a healthy well balanced diet.

Six to seven months

Day 1

7/7.30am	Breast feed or 210–240ml (7–8oz) of formula milk Wheat cereal and milk, with mashed fruit
11.45am/ 12 noon	Chicken risotto (page 69) Drink of water or well-diluted juice from a beaker
2/2.30pm	Breast feed or 150–210ml (5–7oz) of formula milk
5pm	Creamy pasta with spring vegetables (page 70) Drink of water from a beaker
6.30pm	Breast feed or 180–240ml (6–8oz) of formula milk.

Day 2

7/7.30am	Breast feed or 210–240ml (7–8oz) of formula milk Oat cereal with milk and finely chopped fruit
11.45am/ 12 noon	Tuna Pasta (page 71) Drink of water or well-diluted juice from a beaker
2/2.30pm	Breast feed or 150–210ml (5–7oz) of formula milk
5pm	Minestrone soup (page 72) with rice cakes, lightly buttered Drink of water from a beaker

6.30pm   Breast feed or 180–240ml (6–8oz) of formula milk.

Day 3

7/7.30am   Breast feed or 210–240ml (7–8oz) of formula milk
Mixed mashed fruit and yoghurt
Toast, lightly buttered

11.45am/   Quick chicken and vegetable gratin (page 73)
12 noon   Drink of water or well-diluted juice from a beaker

2/2.30pm   Breast feed or 150–210ml (5–7oz) formula milk

5pm   Thick courgette and leek soup (page 74) with mini
sandwiches
Drink of water from a beaker

6.30pm   Breast feed or 180–240ml (6–8oz) of formula milk.

Day 4

7/7.30am   Breast feed or 210–240ml (7–8oz) of formula milk
Wheat cereal with milk and mashed fruit

11.45am/   Chicken casserole (page 75)
12 noon   Drink of water or well-diluted juice from a beaker

2/2.30pm   Breast feed or 150–210ml (5–7oz) of formula milk

5pm   Vegetable broth (page 76) and mini sandwiches
Drink of water from a beaker

6.30pm   Breast feed or 180–240ml (6–8oz) of formula milk.

Day 5

7/7.30am   Breast feed or 210–240ml (7–8oz) of formula milk
Baby muesli with milk

11.45am/   Fish Lyonnaise (page 77) with chopped carrots
12 noon   Drink of water or well-diluted juice from a beaker

2/2.30pm   Breast feed or 150–210ml (5–7oz) of formula milk

5pm   Mixed root medley (page 78)

Drink of water from a beaker

6.30pm   Breast feed or 180–240ml (6–8oz) of formula milk.

Day 6

7/7.30am   Breast feed or 210–240ml (7–8oz) of formula milk
Wheat cereal with milk and mashed fruit

11.45am/   Red lentil savoury (page 79)
12 noon   Drink of water or well-diluted juice from a beaker

2/2.30pm   Breast feed or 150–210ml (5–7oz) of formula milk

5pm   Spotty couscous (page 80)
Drink of water from a beaker

6.30pm   Breast feed or 180–240ml (6–8oz) of formula milk.

Day 7

7/7.30am   Breast feed or 210–240ml (7–8oz) of formula milk
Oat cereal with milk and mashed fruit

11.45am/   Quick chicken and vegetable gratin
12 noon   Drink of water or well-diluted juice from a beaker

2/2.30pm   Breast feed or 150–210ml (5–7oz) of formula or
milk

5pm   Corn chowder (page 81) with rice cakes, lightly
buttered
Drink of water from a beaker

6.30pm   Breast feed or 180–240ml (6–8oz) of formula milk.

*If your baby seems hungry before or following the set mealtimes,
a piece of fruit or yoghurt may be offered at 10am or after lunch.
In the case of a baby still being hungry after his 5pm tea, a yoghurt,
milk pudding or piece of cheese can be offered. However, if he
seems satisfied with his main course, there is no need to offer
these extras.*

Seven to eight months

Day 1

7/7.30am	Breast feed or 210–240ml (7–8oz) of formula milk Wheat cereal with milk and mashed fruit
11.45am/ **12 noon**	Bumper macaroni cheese (page 82) Chopped fruit and yoghurt Drink of water or well-diluted juice from a beaker
2/2.30pm	Breast feed or 150–210ml (5–7oz) of formula milk
5pm	Thick courgette and leek soup with rusks, lightly buttered Drink of water from a beaker
6.30pm	Breast feed or 180–240ml (6–8oz) of formula milk.

Day 2

7/7.30am	Breast feed or 210–240ml (7–8oz) of formula milk Oat cereal with milk and mashed fruit
11.45am/ **12 noon**	Individual fish pie (page 83) and sweetcorn Drink of water or well-diluted juice from a beaker
2/2.30pm	Breast feed or 150–210ml (5–7oz) of formula milk
5pm	Creamy pasta with spring vegetables Drink of water from a beaker
6.30pm	Breast feed or 180–240ml (6–8oz) of formula milk.

Day 3

7/7.30am	Breast feed or 210–240ml (7–8oz) of formula milk Mixed mashed fruit and yoghurt, toast fingers, lightly buttered
11.45am/ **12 noon**	Chicken casserole and green beans Drink of water or well-diluted juice from a beaker
2/2.30pm	Breast feed or 150–210ml (5–7oz) of formula milk

5pm	Baked potato with mashed baked beans Drink of water from a beaker
6.30pm	Breast feed or 180–240ml (6–8oz) of formula milk.

Day 4

7/7.30am	Breast feed or 210–240ml (7–8oz) of formula milk Wheat cereal with milk and finely chopped fruit
11.45am/ 12 noon	Lamb hotpot (page 84) Drink of water or well-diluted juice from a beaker
2/2.30pm	Breast feed or 150–210ml (5–7oz) of formula milk
5pm	Leek and potato soup (page 85) with bread, rusks or rice cakes, lightly buttered Drink of water from a beaker
6.30pm	Breast feed or 180–240ml (6–8oz) of formula milk.

Day 5

7/7.30am	Breast feed or 210–240ml (7–8oz) of formula milk Baby muesli with milk
11.45am/ 12 noon	Chicken risotto Drink of water or well-diluted juice from a beaker
2/2.30pm	Breast feed or 150–210ml (5–7oz) of formula milk
5pm	Corn chowder Drink of water from a beaker
6.30pm	Breast feed or 180–240ml (6–8oz) of formula milk.

Day 6

7/7.30am	Breast feed or 210–240ml (7–8oz) of formula milk Oat cereal with milk and mashed fruit
11.45am/ 12 noon	Fish Lyonnaise, carrots and peas Drink of water or well-diluted juice from a beaker
2/2.30pm	Breast feed or 150–210ml (5–7oz) of formula milk

| 5pm | Vegetable broth and mini sandwiches
Drink of water from a beaker |
| 6.30pm | Breast feed or 180–240ml (6–8oz) of formula milk. |

Day 7

7/7.30am	Breast feed or 210–240ml (7–8oz) of formula milk Mixed mashed fruit and yoghurt, toast fingers, lightly buttered
11.45am/ 12 noon	Individual fish pie and broccoli florets Drink of water or well-diluted juice from a beaker
2/2.30pm	Breast feed or 150–210ml (5–7oz) of formula milk
5pm	Minestrone soup with rice cakes, lightly buttered Drink of water from a beaker
6.30pm	Breast feed or 180–240ml (6–8oz) of formula milk.

*If your baby seems hungry before or following the set mealtimes,
a piece of fruit or yoghurt may be offered at 10am or after lunch.
In the case of a baby still being hungry after his 5pm tea, a yoghurt,
milk pudding or piece of cheese can be offered. However, if he
seems satisfied with his main course, there is no need to offer
these extras.*

Eight to nine months

Day 1

7/7.30am	Breast feed or 210–240ml (7–8oz) of formula milk in a beaker Wheat cereal with milk and finely chopped fruit
11.45am/ 12 noon	Chicken casserole with diced potatoes and broccoli Drink of water or well-diluted juice from a beaker
2/2.30pm	Breast feed or 150–210ml (5–7oz) of formula milk

| 5pm | Thick lentil and carrot soup (page 86) with mini sandwiches
Drink of water from a beaker |
|---|---|
| 6.30pm | Breast feed or 180–240ml (6–8oz) of formula milk. |

Day 2

| 7/7.30am | Breast feed or 210–240ml (7–8oz) of formula milk in a beaker
Oat cereal with milk and grated fruit |
|---|---|
| 11.45am/
12 noon | Vegetable shepherd's pie (page 87)
Drink of water or well-diluted juice from a beaker |
| 2/2.30pm | Breast feed or 150–210ml (5–7oz) of formula milk |
| 5pm | Thick courgette and leek soup with rusks, lightly buttered
Drink of water from a beaker |
| 6.30pm | Breast feed or 180–240ml (6–8oz) of formula milk. |

Day 3

| 7/7.30am | Breast feed or 210–240ml (7–8oz) of formula milk in a beaker
Mixed chopped fruit and yoghurt |
|---|---|
| 11.45am/
12 noon | Lamb hotpot
Drink of water or well-diluted juice from a beaker |
| 2/2.30pm | Breast feed or 150–210ml (5–7oz) of formula milk |
| 5pm | Vegetable broth with mini sandwiches
Drink of water from a beaker |
| 6.30pm | Breast feed or 180–240ml (6–8oz) of formula milk. |

Day 4

7/7.30am	Breast feed or 210–240ml (7–8oz) of formula milk in a beaker

Baby muesli with milk

11.45am/ Fish Lyonnaise with courgettes and carrots
12 noon   Drink of water or well-diluted juice from a beaker

2/2.30pm Breast feed or 150–210ml (5–7oz) of formula milk

5pm   Creamy pasta with spring vegetables
Drink of water from a beaker

6.30pm   Breast feed or 180–240ml (6–8oz) of formula milk.

Day 5

7/7.30am Breast feed or210–240ml (7–8oz) of formula milk in
a beaker
Wheat cereal with milk and mashed fruit

11.45am/ Tuna pasta
12 noon   Drink of water or well-diluted juice from a beaker

2/2.30pm Breast feed or 150–210ml (5–7oz) of formula milk

5pm   Thick courgette and leek soup, with rice cakes,
lightly buttered
Drink of water from a beaker

6.30pm   Breast feed or 180–240ml (6–8oz) of formula milk.

Day 6

7/7.30am Breast feed or 210–240ml (7–8oz) of formula milk
in a beaker
Oat cereal with milk and finely chopped fruit

11.45am/ Quick chicken and vegetable gratin, green beans
12 noon   and diced potatoes
Drink of water or well-diluted juice from a beaker

2/2.30pm Breast feed or 150–210ml (5–7oz) of formula milk

5pm   Spotty couscous
Drink of water from a beaker

6.30pm   Breast feed or 180–240ml (6–8oz) of formula milk.

Day 7

7/7.30am	Breast feed or 210–240ml (7–8oz) of formula milk in a beaker Mixed mashed fruit and yoghurt
11.45am/ **12 noon**	Chicken risotto with chopped Brussels sprouts, cauliflower florets and diced potatoes Drink of water or well-diluted juice from a beaker
2/2.30pm	Breast feed or 150–210ml (5–7oz) of formula milk
5pm	Mixed root medley Drink of water from a beaker
6.30pm	Breast feed or 180–240ml (6–8oz) of formula milk.

If your baby seems hungry before or following the set mealtimes, a piece of fruit or yoghurt may be offered at 10am or after lunch. In the case of a baby still being hungry after his 5pm tea, a yoghurt, milk pudding or piece of cheese can be offered. However, if he seems satisfied with his main course, there is no need to offer these extras.

Emily: aged eight months

Emily had successfully followed the Contented Little Baby routines since she was three weeks old, sleeping through the night from the 10pm feed at eight weeks. When solids were introduced at four months Emily quickly dropped the 10pm feed and slept well from 7pm to 7am. She continued to sleep and eat well until she reached seven months. She then caught a bad cold that lasted for over two weeks and resulted in lots of sleepless nights. She also started to get very fussy about her food, refusing lots of the home-cooked meals that her mother normally gave her. Desperation and concern over her poor appetite and exhaustion from weeks of sleepless nights resulted in Emily's mother giving her commercial baby food at some mealtimes. Once Emily's cold had disappeared her appetite began to improve and she very quickly developed a taste for the jars of baby food. Her mother was so pleased to see her eating normal quantities again that she started using more and more jars.

However, despite getting over her cold and eating well, Emily continued to wake up in the night, and became increasingly difficult to settle. Even when she had the cold Emily had never been fed in the night, although she had been offered cool boiled water. Her mother was convinced that the continued wakings could not be due to hunger, but began to get very worried when Emily started drinking more and more water in the night – on some occasions she could drink as much as 180ml (6oz). On hearing her story I was not convinced that Emily's nutritional needs were being met during the day, as I had seen an increasing incidence of night-time waking in babies of her age who were being fed on jars of commercial baby food.

I explained to Emily's mother that although her daughter was taking the same quantity of commercial food as the amount she was taking of home-made food prior to her cold, the density of the food she was now having was totally different. A huge number of commercial baby meals have a high water content, and include sugar, maltodextrin and other modified starches that are used to thicken and bulk up the ingredients. The jars of chicken and lamb casserole that Emily was eating contained much less protein than the recipes her mother had been cooking for her before she caught her cold.

I convinced Emily's mother to go back to giving her home-cooked meals. However, because Emily had now developed a taste for the commercial baby food we had to re-introduce the home-made versions very slowly. Emily's mother cooked similar recipes to her favourite jar meals, and froze them in quantities of half-to-one ice cubes. She would then very slowly introduce the home-cooked food cubes into the commercial meals, gradually increasing the amount of home-cooked food when she saw that Emily was happy taking it. It took nearly one month to get Emily totally back on to home-cooked food, but during that time her sleeping got better and she had fewer wakings in the night. By the time she was fully on a diet of home-cooked food she was back to sleeping a full 12 hours.

I have dealt with hundreds of problems similar to Emily's. While I believe the occasional use of commercial baby food does not create problems, I am convinced that its over-use may be the cause of poor sleeping habits with some babies.

Your questions answered

Q When will I know if my baby is ready to reduce the number of feeds he is having?

A • The next feed to cut out during the second stage of weaning would be the 11.45am/12 noon feed. Once your baby is having protein at this meal he will not need a milk feed. Using the tier method of feeding (page 25) at this stage will ensure that your baby cuts down on the amount of milk he drinks and increases the solids. I usually find that once a baby is taking between 6 and 8 level tablespoons of food at lunchtime he will be happy to take a drink of cool boiled water or well-diluted juice from a beaker.

Q My baby is six months old and is still taking four full feeds a day. I have tried cutting back on the 11.45am milk feed, but he screams and screams unless he gets a full feed, which results in his refusing solids.

A • Milk is still very important during the second stage of weaning but it would be advisable to try and reduce the amount he is taking at the 11am feed so that he is getting a proper protein lunch by the time he is seven months old.

• It may be that your baby is getting too tired to wait until 11.45am for his lunch, and therefore finds it easier to satisfy his hunger quickly by drinking all his milk first. As he is taking more than his daily milk requirement in his other three feeds, try bringing the feeding time back to 11.30am and offering him his solids first, followed by the milk.

• Alternatively, bring his milk feed time right back to 11am. He will not be quite so hungry so he may well cut back on the amount he drinks, particularly when the amount he eats at breakfast increases. Leave a time space of at least 40 minutes before offering him the solids.

- If he reaches seven months and is still refusing solids, it would be wise to discuss with your health visitor whether this milk feed could be slightly diluted to help improve his appetite for solids. If she agrees, I would suggest that you still give the milk feed slightly earlier than the solids as the very sight of the bottle can be enough to put off some babies of this age eating their solids.

Q When should I introduce a beaker and at which feeds?

A • Once your baby reaches six to seven months of age and is established on a proper protein meal at lunchtime he no longer needs milk at that feed and this would be a good time to introduce a beaker.

- He should be offered cool boiled water or well-diluted juice halfway through the meal and after every few mouthfuls. Many babies take quite a while to get used to drinking from a beaker and will only drink a very small amount in the first few weeks of its introduction. It is important to persevere. Experiment with different types of beaker until you find one that seems to suit your baby.

- If your baby is taking only a very small amount of fluid from a beaker at 11.45am, he may need to be offered extra milk at the 2pm feed or extra cool boiled water later in the day.

- Once he is accustomed to drinking water or well-diluted juice from a beaker, milk can be introduced in a beaker at either the 7am feed or the 2pm feed. This should ideally happen somewhere between the eighth and ninth month, preparing your baby for taking all his drinks from a beaker by one year.

• The COMA report (page 1) recommends that all bottle feeding is stopped by the age of one year, as it can remove the appetite for other foods. In my experience babies who continue milk feeding from a bottle past the age of one year will often refuse milk altogether when the bottle is eventually stopped.

Q When can I introduce cow's milk?

A • The COMA report (page 1) recommends that cow's milk can be introduced in small amounts in the preparation of solid foods from four months, and as a drink from one year. I personally prefer to wait until six months before introducing it in cooking, and if there is a history of allergies, I would wait even longer. If you are unsure about introducing cow's milk into your baby's diet, it would be wise to discuss the matter with your health visitor.

• All cow's milk, whether used in cooking or introduced as a drink at one year, must be full-fat pasteurised milk. Skimmed or semi-skimmed milk is not suitable for children under two years of age. In my opinion it is also advisable to use organic cow's milk.

Q When can I stop puréeing my baby's food?

A • Between six and seven months of age I start to mash or pulse the solids in a food processor. The consistency is not quite so smooth but it is without lumps. Most babies will simply gag on food if they are suddenly expected to go from eating very smooth food to food with lumps in it.

• Once your baby has got used to eating food with slightly more texture I would gradually mash or pulse it less and less until he will take food with lumps in it. By nine months most babies will happily eat food with a range of different textures and consistencies.

- Chicken and meat should still be pulsed very finely until your baby is around 10 months old, or shows signs of being able to chew it easily.

- If your baby refuses food with lumps in it, do not force the issue as it will only create eating problems. Instead make sure that you offer him lots of soft pieces of fruit and vegetables as finger foods. This will ensure that he makes the transition from puréed food to proper food just the same.

Q When can I introduce finger foods?

A
- From six months of age most babies are capable of eating a small amount of finger foods. Get your baby used to sitting in his high chair while you prepare his meal and place a variety of different foods on his tray. At first much of the food will end up on the floor, but if you persist and always offer him a small selection, he will eventually start to eat some of it.

- Start by offering small pieces of softly cooked vegetables or pieces of soft fruit. I find that offering a tablespoon of mixed cooked frozen vegetables is often a successful way of getting babies interested in finger foods. The different colours and textures of the carrots, cauliflowers and peas seem to attract them.

- Once your baby is managing vegetables and fruit, try offering a piece of lightly buttered toast, a low-sugar rusk, rice cake or bread stick.

- Once finger foods are introduced, always wash his hands before and after a meal, and never leave him alone while he is eating.

Recipes for six to nine months

Making your own baby food needn't be fiddly or time-consuming if you make up large quantities at a time and store mini-meals away in the freezer. Build up a selection of small lidded plastic containers for this purpose, and vary the texture of the meals to suit your baby.

All the dishes following can be frozen except where stated. Those unsuitable for freezing make a delicious meal for baby and you. For general freezing and defrosting tips, see pages 13–14.

Chicken risotto

Makes enough for baby and you

Note: Not suitable for freezing

- 1 tbsp **olive oil**
- 200g (7oz) **chicken breast**, skinned, boned, rinsed and cubed
- ½ small **onion**, finely chopped
- 200g (7oz) **risotto rice**
- 250g (9oz) **butternut squash**, peeled, de-seeded and diced
- 2–3 stems fresh **sage**
- 1 litre (1¾ pints) home-made **chicken** or **vegetable stock** (page 46) or filtered **water**

1. Heat the oil in a saucepan. Cook the chicken and onion for 5 minutes or until lightly browned.

2. Add the rice and continue frying for 1–2 minutes or until the rice looks transparent, then add the butternut squash, leaves torn from the sage stems and mix together. Pour over half the stock, stirring frequently. Bring to the boil, then cover, lower the heat and simmer for about 20 minutes, stirring frequently

during cooking and topping up with the remaining stock as needed until all the liquid is absorbed and the rice is creamy and soft or until the desired consistency is reached.

3. Purée in a blender or food processor, blending in batches if necessary, until the desired texture has been reached.

Creamy pasta with spring vegetables

Makes enough for baby and you

Note: Not suitable for freezing

- 150g (5oz) **carrot**, peeled and diced
- 150g (5oz) **broccoli**, cut into small florets, with stems sliced
- 75g (3oz) **green beans**, cut into three
- 75g (3oz) soup or baby **pasta**
- 75g (3oz) mild **Cheddar cheese**, finely grated
- 125–175ml (6–7floz) organic **full-fat milk**

1. Put the carrots in a steamer, cover and cook for 5 minutes.

2. Add the green vegetables and cook for 6–7 minutes or until all the vegetables are just tender and still brightly coloured.

3. Meanwhile, cook pasta in a separate saucepan of boiling filtered water for 6–7 minutes until tender or according to the packet instructions. Drain well.

4. Purée the vegetables and cheese in a blender or food processor, blending in batches if necessary, and gradually adding milk to achieve the desired consistency. Pour the vegetable sauce on top of the pasta.

TIPS

- If preferred, larger pasta shapes can be used instead – just increase the cooking times as necessary.

- As your baby gets older you may like to add a little chopped basil or marjoram to the dish for extra flavour.

- When your baby is happy to move on to coarser textures, continue to purée the vegetable and cream cheese mixture, then mix this with chopped pasta, leaving tiny soup pasta shapes whole.

Tuna pasta

Makes enough for baby and you

Note: Not suitable for freezing

- 50–75g (2–3oz) **pasta shapes**
- 1 tbsp **olive oil**
- 1 small **onion**, finely chopped
- 1 **garlic clove**, crushed
- 2 **tomatoes**, skinned, de-seeded and finely chopped
- 1 tbsp **tomato purée**
- 100ml (3½floz) **apple juice** or filtered **water**
- 200g (7oz) can **tuna** in oil, drained and flaked
- 2–3tbsp **fromage frais**

1. Add the pasta to a pan of boiling filtered water and cook for 10–12 minutes, or according to the packet instructions.
2. Heat the oil in a pan, add the onion and garlic, and cook for 3–4 minutes, stirring all the time.
3. Add the chopped tomatoes, the tomato purée, apple juice or water and the flaked tuna. Cook for a further 4–5 minutes.
4. Stir in enough fromage frais to make a creamy sauce.
5. Drain the pasta and mix with the tuna and sauce.

Minestrone soup
Makes 8–10 servings

- 1 tbsp **olive oil**
- 1 small **onion**, finely chopped
- 1 **garlic clove**, crushed
- 2 sticks **celery**, diced
- 2 **carrots**, peeled and diced
- 1 medium **potato**, peeled and diced
- 200g (7oz) can chopped **tomatoes**
- 1 **courgette**, washed and diced
- 75g (3oz) **green beans**, chopped
- pinch of **dried basil**
- 600ml (1 pint) home-made **chicken** or **vegetable stock** (page 46)
- 200g (7oz) can **haricot beans**, drained and rinsed
- 2tbsp frozen **peas**
- 25g (1oz) small **pasta shapes**

1. Heat the oil in a pan, add the onion and garlic, and cook for 3–4 minutes
2. Add the celery, carrots and potato and cook for a further 5–7 minutes, stirring occasionally.
3. Add the tomatoes, courgette, green beans, basil and stock to the pan, bring to the boil and simmer for about 25 minutes, or until the vegetables are tender.
4. Add the haricot beans, peas and pasta shapes and cook for a further 10–12 minutes.

Quick chicken and vegetable gratin

Makes 4–6 servings

- 1 tbsp **vegetable oil**
- 1 small **carrot**, peeled and diced
- ¼ small **red onion**, diced
- 25g (1oz) **mushrooms**, diced
- 2 tsp **plain flour**
- 4 tbsp **full-fat organic milk**
- 150ml (¼ pint) home-made **chicken** or **vegetable stock** (page 46) or filtered **water**
- 125g (4oz) **cooked chicken**, diced or minced
- 2 tsp finely chopped **fresh herbs**
- 2 tbsp **wholemeal breadcrumbs**
- 3 tbsp mild **Cheddar cheese**, grated
- knob of unsalted **butter**

1. Preheat the oven to 200°C/400°F/gas mark 6.

2. Heat the oil in a large saucepan and fry the carrots, onions and mushrooms together for 5–7 minutes or until softened. Stir in the flour and cook for 1–2 minutes. Gradually stir in the milk and the stock. Bring to the boil then lower the heat and simmer for 5 minutes. Stir in the chicken and the herbs and heat through for 5 minutes.

3. Spoon the chicken and vegetables into a shallow ovenproof dish and sprinkle the breadcrumbs and cheese and dot a little butter evenly over the top. Bake for 15–20 minutes or until golden brown. Serve mashed or puréed.

Thick courgette and leek soup

Makes 8–10 servings

- 1 tbsp **olive oil**
- 300g (10oz) **courgettes**, sliced
- 150g (5oz) **leeks**, chopped
- 2 **potatoes**, peeled and thinly sliced
- 1 **onion**, peeled and thinly sliced
- 2 large **tomatoes**, de-seeded and chopped
- 900ml (1½ pints) home-made **vegetable stock** (page 46) or filtered **water**
- 1 **bay leaf**

1. Heat the oil in a saucepan, add the courgettes, leeks, potatoes and onion and sweat for 3–5 minutes, then add chopped tomatoes, vegetable stock and a bay leaf.

2. Bring to the boil, cover, then lower the heat and simmer for 25 minutes. Remove the bay leaf. Pulse or purée to a smooth texture in a blender or food processor, blending in batches if necessary.

TIPS

- Thick tasty soups make easy-to-eat suppers – ideal if your baby is feeling tired.

- Tomatoes can cause an allergic reaction in some babies, so keep a watchful eye on your baby if introducing them for the first time.

- For older babies, flavour the soup with a sprinkling of fresh, frozen or dried herbs or a tiny amount of garlic and serve with fingers of toast.

Chicken casserole

Makes 6–8 servings

- 1 tbsp **olive oil**
- 1 small **onion**, finely chopped
- 2 organic **chicken breast fillets**, skinned, boned and cubed
- 2 **carrots**, peeled and diced
- 2 **parsnips**, peeled and diced
- 2 medium **potatoes**, peeled and diced
- 300ml (½ pint) home-made **chicken** or **vegetable stock** (page 46)

1. Preheat the oven to 180°C/350°F/gas mark 4.
2. Heat the oil in a pan, add the onion and cook until tender. Add the chicken and cook until sealed on all sides.
3. Transfer the chicken and onion to a casserole dish, add the diced vegetables and pour in the stock. Cover with a lid and cook in the oven for about 45 minutes or until the chicken and vegetables are tender.

Vegetable broth

Makes 8–10 servings

- 2 tbsp **olive oil**
- 1 small **onion**, finely chopped
- 2 **carrots**, peeled and diced
- 1 medium **leek**, finely chopped
- 1 medium **potato**, peeled and diced
- ½ small **turnip**, peeled and diced
- 900ml (1½ pints) homemade **chicken** or **vegetable stock** (page 46)
- 1 medium **carrot**, finely grated

1. Heat the oil in a pan, add the chopped onion and cook for 3–4 minutes.
2. Add the carrots, chopped leek, potato and turnip, and cook for a further 5 minutes.
3. Pour in the stock, bring to the boil and simmer for 30 minutes.
4. Add the grated carrot and simmer for a further 10 minutes, until the vegetables are very tender.

Fish Lyonnaise

Makes 4–6 servings

- 300g (10oz) **potatoes**, peeled and sliced
- 300g (10oz) **cod**, skinned and cubed
- 1 **onion**, very thinly sliced
- 50g (2oz) unsalted **butter**
- 300ml (½ pint) home-made **vegetable stock** (page 46) or filtered **water**
- 125g (4oz) mild **Cheddar cheese**, grated

1. Preheat the oven to 190°C/375°F/gas mark 5.
2. Arrange a layer of sliced potato in the bottom of a casserole dish, then put in a layer of the fish cubes followed by a layer of the sliced onion, dotted with butter. Continue to alternate the layers, finishing with a layer of fish, dotted with butter.
3. Cover with the vegetable stock, top with grated cheese and bake for 20–25 minutes.
4. Served mashed or puréed.

TIPS

- Although cod has very few bones, check carefully when cutting it into cubes to make sure they have all been removed.
- For older babies, mash the finished dish rather than puréeing it and add additional herbs such as a pinch of fresh, dried or frozen tarragon or chives – perhaps even a little tomato purée too.

Mixed root medley

Makes 4–6 servings

- 200g (7oz) **parsnips**, peeled and cubed
- 200g (7oz) **carrots**, peeled and cubed
- 200g (7oz) **swede**, peeled and cubed
- 300g (10oz) **potato**, peeled and cubed
- 450ml (12floz) organic **full-fat milk**
- 150ml (5floz) boiling filtered **water**

1. Put all the vegetables into a saucepan with 300ml (½ pint) milk and the water. Cover and bring to the boil, then lower the heat and simmer for 20–25 minutes, stirring occasionally until the vegetables are tender.

2. Purée in a blender or food processor, blending in batches if necessary, gradually mixing in the remaining milk to achieve the desired consistency.

TIPS

- Cookers vary, so the amount of milk you will need when puréeing may change. If your hob is difficult to turn down to a simmer, you will need all of the milk suggested, as more of the cooking liquid will be driven off during cooking.

- If the root vegetables are very dirty, rinse them again with boiling filtered water when diced.

Red lentil savoury

Makes 4–6 servings

- 75g (3oz) **red lentils**, rinsed
- 150g (5oz) **parsnips**, peeled and cubed
- 225g (8oz) **carrots**, peeled and cubed
- 350g (12oz) **potato**, peeled and cubed
- 600ml (1 pint) home-made **vegetable stock** (page 46) or filtered **water**

1. Put the lentils and root vegetables into a saucepan with the stock or measured water. Bring to the boil, cover, then lower the heat and simmer gently for 40 minutes or until the lentils are soft.

2. Purée in a blender or food processor, blending in batches if necessary, until smooth.

TIPS

- Wash the red lentils before use – they can be surprisingly dusty.

- As your baby gets older and more adventurous, try adding a pinch of ground turmeric, coriander and cumin to the recipe for extra flavour.

- Use butternut squash instead of the parsnip or carrot, if liked.

Spotty couscous

Makes enough for baby and you

Note: Not suitable for freezing

- ½ **orange** or **red pepper**, de-seeded and finely diced
- 50g (2oz) **courgette**, finely diced
- 50g (2oz) **green beans**, finely sliced
- 50g (2oz) canned or frozen **sweetcorn**
- 100g (3½oz) **couscous**
- 2 tbsp **sultanas** or **raisins**
- 2 tsp **olive oil**
- 250ml (8floz) boiling filtered **water**
- 4 tbsp freshly squeezed **orange juice**

1. Cook the vegetables in a steamer for 5 minutes or until tender.
2. Meanwhile, put the couscous into a bowl with the sultanas, oil and boiling water. Cover with a plate and leave to absorb water for 5 minutes. Add the orange juice and fluff up with a fork.
3. Dice or mash the vegetables to the baby's desired texture. Stir into the couscous and spoon into bowls.

TIP

- This easy supper is ideal for slightly older children and parents too. If making for the whole family, add seasoning once the baby's portion has been dished up.
- If you have mint growing in the garden, chop a little and stir into the dish before serving.
- Fresh orange juice not only adds flavour, but the vitamin C it contains helps iron and calcium to be absorbed by the body.

Corn chowder

Makes 6–8 servings

- 350g (12oz) **potato**, peeled and diced
- 100g (3½oz) **carrot**, peeled and diced
- 1 small **onion**, finely chopped
- 450ml (12floz) organic **full-fat milk**
- 1 **bay leaf**
- 75g (3oz) frozen **sweetcorn**

1. Put all the ingredients except the sweetcorn into a saucepan. Bring to the boil, cover, then lower the heat and simmer for 10–12 minutes or until the vegetables are tender.
2. Add the sweetcorn to the pan and cook for 5 more minutes.
3. Discard the bay leaf, then purée the milk and vegetable mixture in a blender or food processor, blending in batches if necessary, until the desired consistency has been reached.

TIPS

- As your baby grows, simply mash the ingredients together and serve as a chunky soup-style meal with toast fingers.
- Canned sweetcorn can be used but make sure it has been processed without salt or sugar.

Bumper macaroni cheese

Makes 4 servings

- 100g (3½oz) **soup pasta**
- 25g (1oz) unsalted **butter**
- 25g (1oz) **plain flour**
- 350–400ml (12–14floz) organic **full-fat milk**
- 75g (3oz) fresh **young leaf spinach**
- 75g (3oz) mild **Cheddar cheese,** grated
- a little grated **nutmeg**

1. Cook the pasta in a saucepan of boiling water for 6–7 minutes (or according to packet instructions) until soft.

2. Meanwhile, melt the butter in a second saucepan, stir in the flour then gradually mix in 350ml (12floz) milk and bring to the boil, stirring until thickened and smooth. If too thick, add a little more milk.

3. Drain the pasta into a sieve, rinse and dry the pan. Wash the spinach well, shake off most of the water, then add to the dried pan and cook for 1–2 minutes until just wilted.

4. Take the spinach out of the pan, finely chop and stir into the sauce along with the cheese and nutmeg. Depending on the size of the pasta, finely chop or mash it to suit your baby.

TIPS

- As the pasta swells with standing, adjust the consistency with extra milk when reheating.

- Spinach can be a little strong-tasting on its own, so mix with a cheesy sauce to make it more acceptable for young diners.

Individual fish pies

Makes 6 servings

- 15g (½oz) unsalted **butter**
- 1 small **onion**, finely chopped
- 1 medium **leek**, thinly sliced
- 300g (10oz) **white fish fillets**, skinned
- 1 tbsp **plain flour**
- 300 ml (½ pint) organic **full-fat milk**
- 75g (3oz) mild **Cheddar cheese**, grated
- 25g (1oz) fresh white or brown **breadcrumbs**

1. Preheat the oven to 200°C/400°F/gas mark 6.
2. Melt the butter in a pan and sweat the onions and leeks for 3–4 minutes.
3. Cut the fish into cubes and place in small, lightly greased ramekins.
4. Stir the flour into the vegetables and cook for 2–3 minutes. Gradually add the milk, stirring all the time. Cook for a further 1–2 minutes until the sauce begins to thicken. Stir in 50g (2oz) of the cheese, then spoon the mixture over the fish.
5. Mix the breadcrumbs and the remaining cheese together, then sprinkle on top of each filled ramekin. Bake for 20 minutes until lightly golden and the fish is cooked.

Lamb hotpot

Makes 4–6 servings

- 250g (9oz) lean **lamb fillet**
- 1 tbsp **olive oil**
- ½ small **red onion**, chopped
- 300ml (½ pint) home-made **vegetable stock** (page 46) or filtered **water**
- pinch of dried **mixed herbs** or 2 tsp finely chopped **fresh herbs**
- 125g (4oz) **carrots**, peeled and diced
- 125g (4oz) **swede**, peeled and diced
- 125g (4oz) **potato**, peeled and diced

1. Wash the lamb under running cold water, dry with kitchen towel and cut into small cubes.
2. Heat the oil in a casserole dish and fry the lamb with the onion until the meat is browned.
3. Stir in the stock and herbs, add the vegetables and bring to the boil. Cover the casserole dish and simmer for 30 minutes.
4. Serve mashed or puréed.

TIPS

- If you have the oven on, cooking for the rest of the family, then this dish can also be casseroled at 180°C/350°F/gas mark 4 for 1–1¼ hours.
- For older babies, chop the finished dish or for toddlers, add tiny bite-sized dumplings.

Leek and potato soup

Makes 8–10 servings

- 25g (1oz) unsalted **butter**
- 450g (1lb) **leeks**, chopped
- 450g (1lb) **potatoes**, peeled and sliced
- 1 small **onion**, thinly sliced
- 1.1 litres (2 pints) home-made **vegetable stock** (page 46) or filtered **water**

1. Heat the butter in a saucepan. Add the vegetables and sweat for 3–5 minutes, then add vegetable stock. Bring to the boil, then lower the heat and simmer, uncovered, for approximately 25 minutes. Purée to a smooth texture in a blender or food processor, blending in batches if necessary.

2. If necessary, add full-fat cow's milk to achieve the right consistency.

TIPS

- If you are worried about the amount of milk your child is drinking, use half-stock and half-milk in this recipe, or stir in some fromage frais or full-fat cream cheese after puréeing.

- Tired children find soup very comforting, and it can be quickly reheated – ideal if you have been out for the afternoon and need tea in a hurry.

- Serve with strips of toast or puff pastry shapes sprinkled with grated cheese as finger foods.

Thick lentil and carrot soup

Makes 6–8 servings

- 1 tbsp **olive oil**
- 1 small **onion**, peeled and thinly sliced
- 2 **carrots**, peeled and thinly sliced
- 1 **garlic** clove, peeled and chopped
- 200g (7oz) **red lentils**
- 1.1 litre (2 pints) home-made **vegetable stock** (page 46) or filtered **water**

1. Heat the oil in a large saucepan, add the onion, carrots and garlic, if using. Sweat for 3–5 minutes then add lentils and vegetable stock.
2. Bring to the boil, then cover, lower the heat and simmer for 30–35 minutes.
3. Purée to a smooth texture in a blender or food processor, blending in batches if necessary.

TIPS

- Red lentils make a great store-cupboard standby as they don't require pre-soaking like the other larger pulses and provide a good source of protein.
- For adventurous children you may also like to add a little ground cumin and coriander when cooking the lentils.

Vegetable shepherd's pie

Makes 6–8 servings

- 125g (4oz) unsalted **butter**
- 125g (4oz) **leeks**, trimmed, washed and finely chopped
- 1 **red onion**, finely chopped
- 175g (6oz) split **red lentils**
- about 500ml (18floz) home-made **vegetable stock** (page 46) or boiling filtered **water**
- 2 **tomatoes**, skinned and chopped
- 1 tsp dried **mixed herbs**
- 4 tbsp fresh **lemon juice**
- 900g (1¾lb) floury **potatoes**, peeled and cut into chunks
- 75g (3oz) mild **Cheddar cheese**, finely grated

1. Melt 50g (2oz) butter in a saucepan, add the leeks and onion and cook for about 8–10 minutes until softened.

2. Add the lentils and stir for 1–2 minutes to cover the lentils in the fat.

3. Add the stock or water, bring to the boil, then reduce the heat, half cover with a lid and simmer for about 15 minutes or until the lentils are soft, stirring occasionally. (There should be a little free liquid, so stir over a high heat to drive off any excess.) Cool slightly.

4. Remove the saucepan from the heat and stir in the tomatoes, herbs and lemon juice. Leave to cool.

5   Meanwhile, cook the potates in boiling water for 20 minutes or until tender. Drain well, then mash until smooth. Beat in the remaining butter and the cheese.

6.   Preheat the oven to 200°C/400°F/gas mark 6.

7.   Spoon the vegetable and lentil mixture into a 1.2-litre/2-pint shallow oven-proof dish and level the surface. Spoon over the mashed potato.

8.   Bake for 20–25 minutes until the topping is crisp and golden.

9.   To serve, leave to cool slightly, then mash with a fork.

Third Stage Weaning: nine to twelve months

4

By the third stage of weaning your baby should be adopting a more adult style of eating. Most food should now be served mashed, chopped or diced, as it is important that he learns to chew properly at this stage. Once he has mastered the art of chewing lightly cooked vegetables and bite-sized pieces of soft fruit, try introducing raw vegetables and salads into his diet. A small amount of finger foods should be introduced at every meal and he should be encouraged to feed himself from the spoon, even if it means that meals take longer and he gets messier while eating. Eating should always be a pleasure for your baby and it is important that you allow him to take control of his eating habits at this stage, which often means that he will eat better at some meals than others. By the time he reaches one year of age he should be eating and enjoying a wide variety of food from the different food groups – carbohydrates, fruit and vegetables and protein. It is important to continue to limit foods that are high in sugar and salt.

Breakfast

By the time your baby reaches one year he should be taking all his drinks from a beaker, so try to get him used to drinking some of his breakfast milk from a beaker by the time he reaches nine months. Once he is taking all his milk from a beaker the amount he drinks will probably go down to around 120–150ml (4–5oz), with 60–90ml (2–3oz) on his breakfast cereal. Some babies go through a stage of refusing their breakfast cereal at this age. If this happens, try offering yoghurt and fruit instead, followed by toast and butter or a fruit spread. Scrambled egg can also be offered once or twice a week.

Lunch

I have always found it better to give my babies their daily serving of protein at lunchtime as opposed to teatime. Babies of this age can often get very tired and irritable by 5pm and be a bit more fussy about eating. If they have had a well-balanced meal of protein and vegetables at lunchtime, you can be relaxed about what they have at tea-time. If, for some reason, your baby doesn't have his daily serving of protein at lunchtime, include some grated cheese for tea.

Vegetables should be lightly steamed and chopped. Try to ensure that you vary the selection from day to day so that your baby is aware of the different colours and textures. It is also important not to overload his plate at this stage – an overfull plate can put some babies off, and with others can lead to a game of throwing food on the floor. Serve up a small amount and if he finishes it, offer more. If he does start to play up at mealtimes, refusing to eat or throwing his food on the floor, remove the plate immediately. It is very important not to get into a habit of force feeding or cajoling your baby to eat. Babies of this age very quickly learn to fuss and refuse their main course if they know they will be offered a treat such as fromage frais or a biscuit. If your baby doesn't eat well at lunchtime, offer him a piece of fruit or cheese mid-afternoon to see him through to teatime. A very hungry baby may need a serving of fruit and yoghurt in addition to his savoury lunch.

A drink of well-diluted, pure unsweetened orange or apple juice will help the absorption of iron at this meal. However, it is very important to try to get your baby to have most of his solids before offering him a drink. Allowing him to drink too much before his meal may considerably reduce his appetite.

By the end of the first year your baby should be able to eat much the same as the rest of the family and it is important that some of his meals are integrated with yours as this is how he will learn his table manners. When preparing family meals cook without salt, sugar and unnecessary additives, reserve the baby's portion, then add the desired flavourings for the rest of the family.

Tea

During the weaning stage your baby should be offered a wide variety of finger foods and teatime is the ideal meal to do this. Savoury sandwiches, small pieces of pizza and chopped up vegetarian sausages are good examples of finger foods that can be given – served, say, with a thick soup, vegetable lasagne or vegetable bake. Many babies will cut right back or refuse their 2.30pm feed altogether at this stage. If you find that your baby's milk intake has dropped below 500ml (18oz) introduce foods such as cheesy vegetable bakes, mini quiches, baked potatoes with grated cheese or vegetables and pasta in a milk sauce at teatime. Fromage frais and milk puddings can also be offered at teatime if you are concerned about your baby's milk intake.

By one year of age your baby's minimum daily milk requirement will drop to 350ml (12oz) and the bedtime bottle should be replaced with a drink from a beaker. To get him used to less milk at this last feed offer him a small amount from a beaker with his tea, followed by a drink of 150–180ml (5–6oz) from a beaker at bedtime.

Daily requirements

During the third stage of weaning it is important that you encourage your baby to take all his milk from a beaker. The COMA report (page 1) says that large volumes of milk should be discouraged after one year as they can take away the baby's appetite for solid food. COMA recommends that no more than 600ml (20oz) a day inclusive of milk used in food should be allowed. The majority of babies will be having two to three milk drinks a day at one year of age and need a minimum of 350ml (12oz) of milk each day, inclusive of milk used in cooking and on cereal.

By the age of one year your baby should be enjoying three well-balanced meals a day and be able to join in most of the family meals. Some babies may also need a snack mid-morning or afternoon – try to offer healthy foods, avoiding biscuits, cakes and crisps.

Weaning guidelines

- Between the ages of nine and twelve months your baby should have three to four servings of carbohydrates a day in the form of cereals, wholemeal bread, pasta or potatoes.

- Your baby also needs three to four portions of fruit and vegetables, ideally taking more vegetables than fruit. By the end of the first year he should be eating a wide variety of raw and salad vegetables. The majority of his fruit and vegetables should now be offered chopped, sliced or cubed, instead of being mashed or puréed.

- Your baby will also need one serving of approximately 50g (2oz) animal protein a day or two servings of vegetable protein a day. Continue to avoid meats such as ham and bacon which are high in salt. Depending on how many teeth your baby has, most meat, poultry and fish should be chopped up into small pieces instead of being minced or mashed.

- Babies are very aware of colour and texture at this stage, so try to make food look appealing and interesting. Avoid mashing and mixing his different foods together, and make up a two-week menu plan to help you avoid giving the same foods too close together.

- If your baby is not taking his daily milk requirements between two or three feeds, increase the amount of cheese and yoghurt you give him. Also offer more sauces and puddings using milk.

- At mealtimes it is best to serve water or well-diluted pure fruit juice *after* your baby has eaten most of his solids so that the edge will not be taken off his appetite.

Feeding plan
at nine to twelve months

Parents and carers should use this plan as a guide. All babies differ, so don't feel anxious if your child doesn't seem to like a particular food or seems to want a little more or less. Be guided by your baby.

Foods to introduce

Stronger-tasting fruit and vegetables such as aubergine, beetroot, cucumber, garlic, pineapple, fresh berry fruits and high-fibre dried fruits such as prunes and figs; small amounts of unsweetened orange juice, diluted one part to 10 parts water; stronger-tasting beef and liver, but offer liver in tiny amounts and just once a week; wider use of herbs and spices, but still in small amounts.

Week one

Day 1

7/7.30am	Breast feed or a drink of formula milk from a beaker Wheat cereal with milk and finely chopped fruit
11.45am/ 12 noon	Fishy ribbons (page 104) and mixed vegetables Drink of water or well-diluted juice from a beaker
2/2.30pm	Breast feed or a drink of formula milk, water or well-diluted juice from a beaker
5pm	Vegetable broth with mini sandwiches,
6.30pm	Breast feed or 180ml (6oz) of formula milk.

Day 2

7/7.30am	Breast feed or a drink of formula milk from a beaker Oat cereal with milk and finely chopped fruit

11.45am/	Mini moussaka (page 105)
12 noon	Drink of water or well-diluted juice from a beaker
2/2.30pm	Breast feed or a drink of formula milk, water or well-diluted juice from a beaker
5pm	Leek and potato soup plus mini sandwiches
6.30pm	Breast feed or 180ml (6oz) of formula milk.

Day 3

7/7.30am	Breast feed or a drink of formula milk from a beaker Fruit yoghurt and toast fingers, lightly buttered
11.45am/ **12 noon**	Lamb and vegetable casserole (page 107) and creamed potatoes Drink of water or well-diluted juice from a beaker
2/2.30pm	Breast feed or a drink of formula milk, water or well-diluted juice from a beaker
5pm	Pizza potatoes (page 108)
6.30pm	Breast feed or 180ml (6oz) of formula milk.

Day 4

7/7.30am	Breast feed or a drink of formula milk from a beaker Scrambled egg on toast
11.45am/ **12 noon**	Mini salmon skewers (page 109) Drink of water or well-diluted juice from a beaker
2/2.30pm	Breast feed or a drink of formula milk, water or well-diluted juice from a beaker
5pm	Mixed vegetable frittata (page 110)
6.30pm	Breast feed or 180ml (6oz) of formula milk.

Day 5

7/7.30am	Breast feed or drink of formula milk from a beaker Muesli with milk
11.45am/ 12 noon	Chicken-peach casserole (page 111) Drink of water or well-diluted juice from a beaker
2/2.30pm	Breast feed or a drink of formula milk, water or well-diluted juice from a beaker
5pm	Chinese noodles (page 112)
6.30pm	Breast feed or 180ml (6oz) of formula milk.

Day 6

7/7.30am	Breast feed or drink of formula milk from a beaker Wheat cereal with milk and finely chopped fruit
11.45am/ 12 noon	Chicken with sweet peppers (page 113), Brussels sprouts and boiled potatoes Drink of water or well-diluted juice from a beaker
2/2.30pm	Breast feed or a drink of formula milk, water or well-diluted juice from a beaker
5pm	Corn chowder
6.30pm	Breast feed or 180ml (6oz) of formula milk.

Day 7

7/7.30am	Breast feed or drink of formula milk from a beaker Oat cereal with milk and finely chopped fruit
11.45am/ 12 noon	Chicken and butter bean burgers (page 114) Drink of water or well-diluted juice from a beaker
2/2.30pm	Breast feed or a drink of formula milk, water or well-diluted juice from a beaker
5pm	Chinese noodles
6.30pm	Breast feed or 180ml (6oz) of formula milk.

Week two

Day 8

7/7.30am	Breast feed or drink of formula milk from a beaker Wheat cereal with milk and finely chopped fruit
11.45am/ 12 noon	Fish fingers, mixed vegetables and diced potatoes Drink of water or well-diluted juice from a beaker
2/2.30pm	Breast feed or a drink of formula milk, water or well-diluted juice from a beaker
5pm	Minestrone soup with rice cakes, lightly buttered
6.30pm	Breast feed or 180ml (6oz) of formula milk.

Day 9

7/7.30am	Breast feed or drink of formula milk from a beaker Oat cereal with milk and finely chopped fruit
11.45am/ 12 noon	Mini moussaka Drink of water or well-diluted juice from a beaker
2/2.30pm	Breast feed or a drink of formula milk, water or well-diluted juice from a beaker
5pm	Thick lentil and carrot soup with mini sandwiches
6.30pm	Breast feed or 180ml (6oz) of formula milk.

Day 10

7/7.30am	Breast feed or drink of formula milk from a beaker Scrambled eggs on toast
11.45am/ 12 noon	Chicken and mushroom stir-fry (page 115) Drink of water or well-diluted juice from a beaker
2/2.30pm	Breast feed or a drink of formula milk, water or well-diluted juice from a beaker

5pm	Baked beans on mashed potatoes
6.30pm	Breast feed or 180ml (6oz) of formula milk.

Day 11

7/7.30am	Breast feed or drink of formula milk from a beaker Yoghurt with finely chopped fruit and toast fingers, lightly buttered
11.45am/ 12 noon	Beef and barley pot supper (page 116) with broccoli Drink of water or well-diluted juice from a beaker
2/2.30pm	Breast feed or a drink of formula milk, water or well-diluted juice from a beaker
5pm	Minestrone soup with rice cakes, lightly buttered
6.30pm	Breast feed or 180ml (6oz) of formula milk.

Day 12

7/7.30am	Breast feed or drdink of formula milk from a beaker Baby muesli with milk
11.45am/ 12 noon	Chicken and vegetable oat crumble (page 117) Drink of water or well-diluted juice from a beaker
2/2.30pm	Breast feed or a drink of formula milk, water or well-diluted juice from a beaker
5pm	Pizza potatoes and mixed salad
6.30pm	Breast feed or 180ml (6oz) of formula milk.

Day 13

7/7.30am	Breast feed or drink of formula milk from a beaker Wheat cereal with milk and finely chopped fruit
11.45am/ 12 noon	Kiddies' kedgeree (page 118) Drink of water or well-diluted juice from a beaker

2/2.30pm	Breast feed or a drink of formula milk, water or well-diluted juice from a beaker
5pm	Chinese noodles and mixed salad
6.30pm	Breast feed or 180ml (6oz) of formula milk.

Day 14

7/7.30am	Breast feed or drink of formula milk from a beaker Oat cereal with milk and finely chopped fruit
11.45am/ 12 noon	Baby Bolognese (page 119), green beans and sweetcorn Drink of water or well-diluted juice from a beaker
2/2.30pm	Breast feed or a drink of formula milk, water or well-diluted juice from a beaker
5pm	Pick-up sticks (page 120)
6pm	Breast feed or 180ml (6oz) of formula milk.

At this stage it is important that your baby receives sufficient fruit. This should be offered mid-morning and mid-afternoon. If your baby still seems hungry in advance of the set mealtimes, yoghurt may be offered after lunch or mid-afternoon. However, if he seems satisfied with his main course, there is no need to offer this.

Theo: aged 11 months

Theo had always been a good feeder, enjoying a wide range of freshly cooked foods. At around eight months his mother noticed he was starting to reject more and more of his favourite meals. By the time she contacted me Theo had reached 10 months and meal-times had become a complete battleground, with him clamping his mouth shut the minute a spoon was put anywhere near his mouth. His mother would try lots of different tactics to try and get him back to his old eating habits. She would spend ages singing, clapping and playing all sorts of games at mealtimes to try and get Theo to smile so he would take just one extra mouthful. If this approach failed she would then try offering him endless different choices of meals, with him often taking no more than a mouthful from each choice.

When I received Theo's food diary I could see that there were several very obvious things that were not helping his feeding problems. One was the timing of his drinks, which were too close to mealtimes and taking the edge off his appetite; another was the fact that Theo was still drinking his morning and evening milk from a bottle. He was consuming over 240ml (8oz) at both of these feeds, which was also taking the edge off his appetite.

I advised Theo's mother to offer him no more than 180ml (6oz) from a beaker first thing in the morning and no more than 200ml (7oz) from his bottle in the evening. These amounts, along with milk used in cereals, would still exceed 350ml (12oz), the minimum recommended at one year of age. Any other fluid should be offered midway between meals, not an hour before. At mealtimes I advised that Theo should not be given his juice until he had eaten at least half of his solids.

It was also obvious from the food diary that most of Theo's food was still being mashed and mixed up and that very little finger food was being offered. I explained that babies of Theo's age become interested in the colour, texture and shape of their food and I suspected he had become very bored with all his food still being mashed and mixed up into one bowl. It was very important that he should be offered a selection of finger foods at most meals and that he should be allowed to feed himself, regardless of how messy he got.

Although I advise offering a selection of finger foods the choice should not be endless. At this age the amount a baby eats at individual meals can become very erratic and it is best never to try to force the baby to feed. Allow a certain length of time but if it becomes obvious that he is not interested, clear the food away. He should not be coaxed or cajoled into eating – all babies will eat well if they are hungry enough and not over-tired. It is best to judge a baby's food intake over several days at this age, not at what he eats at individual meals.

Theo's feeding did improve considerably although he still had days when he was fussy. As he had just started learning to walk, I suspected that tiredness might also be a cause of his fussiness and I advised his mother to start his meals slightly earlier on days when he had been extremely energetic.

Your questions answered

Q My baby is nine months old and has happily had three milk feeds a day of approximately 175–200ml (6–7oz) of formula each since he was six months old. He is now getting very fussy and fretful at his bedtime bottle, sometimes taking as little as 90ml (3oz), which has resulted in him waking earlier than 7am looking for a feed. I have tried cutting back on his 2.30pm feed but he gets very irritable and looks for his tea nearer 4.30pm instead of 5pm.

A • Many babies do cut back or refuse a third milk feed at this stage. Obviously it is better if it is the mid-afternoon feed and not the last feed of the day. Continue to give your baby a reduced feed in the middle of the day but try offering him it at 3pm instead of 2.30pm and bring his tea forward to 4.45pm. Once he has increased his bedtime feed for several days you can try pushing his tea-time solids back to 5pm. Do this gradually by two or three minutes every three days.

- If the above doesn't work it is also worthwhile looking at the amount of solids you are giving your baby at teatime. If he is having in excess of 8 tablespoons of solids, try cutting back slightly, as this is another cause of babies cutting back too hard on their bedtime milk feed.

- Another reason for cutting back on the bedtime milk feed is over-tiredness. It is at this age that many babies are beginning to crawl and pull themselves up. This extra physical activity can make them become very overtired at bedtime. It may be that your baby needs an extra 15 minutes' sleep at lunchtime so that he doesn't become overtired at bedtime. If he refuses the extra sleep you may find that bringing his bed-time routine forward by 15 minutes will help.

- If none of the above works, I would try cutting out the mid-afternoon milk feed altogether and replacing it with a drink of well-diluted juice or water and a snack, so he can get through to tea-time. If he then drinks 180ml (6oz) in the morning and 180ml (6oz) in the evening, he will have reached the minimum amount. Extra milk on his cereal and in cooking should then easily meet his requirements.

Q My baby is nearly 14 months of age and has happily drunk his milk in the morning and mid-afternoon from a beaker for over two months now. But he screams when I try to give him milk from a beaker at bedtime. He is taking nearly 240ml (8oz) at bed-time from the bottle and around 180ml (6oz) from the beaker first thing in the morning and mid-afternoon. He has also started to get very fussy

about his solids at breakfast, and on occasion has refused them altogether.

A • During the third stage of weaning many babies will automatically cut out their third milk feed. When a baby continues to have three milk feeds at this age but starts to refuse solids it would be wise to gradually reduce the third feed, which should always be the mid-afternoon feed.

• Gradually reduce the amount you give your baby to drink at 2.30pm and offer him a drink of milk from a beaker with his teatime solids instead. This should enable you gradually to reduce the amount he drinks from a bottle at bedtime.

• After a couple of weeks when he is used to taking a small drink of milk from a beaker at tea-time and his bedtime bottle is reduced to 150–180ml (5–6oz), try offering him that amount from a beaker.

• At this age it often helps if parents have a drink from a beaker too, or if a favourite teddy is offered a drink from a beaker.

Q When can I give cow's milk as a drink?

A • Cow's milk can be given to drink once your baby reaches one year of age. It should always be full-fat and pasteurised. If possible, try to give your baby organic cow's milk as it comes from cows fed exclusively on grass.

• If your baby refuses cow's milk, I would try mixing it with formula: simply replace 25g (1oz) of milk with formula. Gradually increase the proportion of cow's milk while decreasing the infant formula, until your child is drinking cow's milk only. If your child continues to refuse cow's milk, try a follow-on milk that tastes similar and can be used up to two years of age.

Q **When should I encourage my baby to feed himself from the spoon?**

A • By the time they reach 12 months, the majority of babies will be capable of getting some of their food into their mouth using their spoon. Spoon-feeding will be made easier for your baby if the food is served in a bowl as opposed to a plate.

• Once your baby is capable of feeding himself with a spoon mealtimes will probably take longer so allow extra time. Always supervise your baby during mealtimes. Never, ever leave him alone.

• Mealtimes can become extra messy once your baby is self-feeding. It is very important to remain very patient at this stage – the most important thing is that he eats well, regardless of how he gets the food into his mouth.

Recipes for nine to twelve months and over

As your baby's taste develops, you can begin to cook for all the family. However, you need to remember not to add any salt to the meals until you have set aside your baby's portion. Note that recipes unsuitable for freezing make one serving each for baby and you.

Fishy ribbons

Makes 2 servings

- 125g (4oz) **cod or haddock fillet**, skinned and rinsed
- 1 **egg**
- 40g (1½oz) fresh white or brown **breadcrumbs**
- 1 tbsp freshly grated **Parmesan cheese** (optional)
- 1 tbsp **sunflower oil**

1. Cut the fish into finger-sized strips. Beat the egg on a plate. Mix the breadcrumbs and Parmesan, if using, on another plate. Dip the fish strips into the egg and roll in crumbs until well coated. Put on a plate, cover and chill for at least 30 minutes.

2. When ready to cook heat the oil in a frying pan, add the fish strips a few at a time and cook for 3–4 minutes, turning several times until the breadcrumbs are golden brown and the fish turns white and flakes easily.

3. Drain the fish on to kitchen paper.

TIPS

- Use this same idea to make chicken ribbons, using strips of boneless, skinless chicken breast fillet.
- If serving with ketchup, go for the low-sugar and low-salt varieties.

Mini moussaka

Makes 4 servings

- 250g (9oz) lean minced **lamb**
- 1 small **onion**, finely chopped
- 100g (3½oz) **aubergine**, diced
- 1 clove **garlic**, crushed
- 175g (6oz) **courgette**, diced
- 300g (10oz) **passata** or finely chopped **tomatoes**
- 300ml (½ pint) filtered **water**
- pinch of ground **cinnamon** and **allspice**

Topping:

- 350g (12oz) baking **potatoes**, peeled
- 1 tbsp unsalted **butter**
- 1 tbsp **plain flour**
- 150ml (¼ pint) organic **full-fat milk**
- 25g (1oz) mild **Cheddar cheese**, grated
- 1 tbsp freshly grated **Parmesan cheese**

1. Preheat the oven to 200°C/400°F/gas mark 6.
2. Dry-fry the mince, onion and aubergine together until browned. Stir in the garlic and courgette, then add the passata, water and spices. Cover and bring to the boil, stirring, then lower the heat and simmer for 35 minutes.
3. Meanwhile, thinly slice the potatoes and cook in boiling filtered water for 4–5 minutes or until just tender. Drain well.
4. Put the butter, flour and milk into a small saucepan and bring to the boil, whisking continuously until thickened and smooth. Stir in the Cheddar cheese and set aside.

5. Divide the mince mixture between 4 small ovenproof dishes. Pour some cheese sauce over each one. Arrange potatoes over the top and sprinkle with Parmesan. Cool and freeze at this stage.

6. Bake for 25 minutes or until the top is golden brown. Serve with just cooked green beans or broccoli florets.

TIPS

• The mince mixture can be casseroled in the oven at 180°C/350°F/gas mark 4 for 1¼ hours, if preferred.

• Minced beef can be used if preferred, but it will have a stronger taste.

• The mince mixture and sauce can also be turned into child-sized portions of lasagne by layering with no-soak pasta sheets. Add a little extra water or stock at the end of cooking, as the lasagne will absorb some of the liquid.

• Passata is sold in jars alongside the other Italian products in the supermarket, but you could use canned chopped tomatoes instead.

Lamb and vegetable casserole

Makes 4–6 servings

- 250g (9oz) lean **lamb fillet**, cubed
- 25g (1oz) unsalted **butter**
- 1 large **carrot**, peeled and diced
- 1 **leek**, washed and thinly sliced
- 300ml (½ pint) home-made **vegetable stock** (page 46) or filtered **water**
- 420g (14oz) can chopped **tomatoes**
- pinch of mixed **dried herbs** or 2 tsp chopped **fresh herbs**

1. Wash the lamb under cold running water and pat dry with kitchen towel.
2. Heat the butter in a casserole dish, and fry lamb until browned all over. Add the carrot and leek and cook for 5 minutes, then add the stock, chopped tomatoes and herbs. Bring to the boil, cover, then lower the heat and simmer for 30–40 minutes.
3. Serve mashed or finely chopped with pasta or rice.

TIPS

- Home-made chicken or vegetable stock (page 46) could be added instead of tomatoes along with a sprinkling of red lentils or butter beans.

- Many supermarkets sell packs of lean diced lamb but they can be expensive and only available in 450g (1lb) packs. Fillet of lamb is often sold in smaller amounts and is extremely tender.

Pizza potatoes

Makes 4 servings

- 4 small **baking potatoes**, scrubbed
- 100g (3½oz) **mozzarella cheese**, coarsely grated
- 1 **tomato**, skinned and finely chopped
- 1 tsp **tomato purée**
- 1 tbsp finely chopped fresh **basil** (optional)
- 3–4 tbsp organic **full-fat milk**

1. Preheat the oven to 200°C/400°F/gas mark 6. Prick the potatoes and oven bake for 50–60 minutes or until soft.

2. Cut the potatoes in half, scoop out the soft centres and mash on a plate with three-quarters of the cheese, the chopped tomato, the tomato purée, basil (if using) and enough milk to make a creamy mash.

3. Spoon the mixture back into the potato shells. Sprinkle with the remaining cheese. Reheat when needed at the same temperature as in step 1 for 20 minutes until piping hot. Cool to desired temperature for your baby and check before serving.

TIPS

- Don't give potato skins to your baby as they will still be too tricky to chew – they have really only been included here as mini containers.

- As your baby gets more adventurous, try adding other ingredients such as sweetcorn, diced mushrooms or courgettes.

- Adapt the idea to make just one potato as an easy store cupboard supper with whatever mild cheese you may have, plus a few frozen mixed vegetables or frozen well-drained spinach.

Mini salmon skewers

Makes 4 servings

- 350g (12oz) baking **potatoes**, cut into chunks
- 250g (9oz) **butternut squash**, de-seeded, peeled and diced
- 250g (9oz) **salmon fillet**, skin removed
- juice of ½ **lime**
- 2 tbsp organic **full-fat milk**
- 15g (½oz) unsalted **butter**
- cooked **broccoli florets**, to serve

1. Half fill the bottom of a two-tier steamer with boiling water, add potatoes to the base and the squash to the top. Cover and steam the squash for10 minutes, the potatoes for 15 minutes, or until tender.

2. Meanwhile, cut the fish into small squares, carefully checking for and removing any bones. Thread on to 8 wooden cocktail sticks. Squeeze lime juice over and set aside.

3. When the vegetables are cooked, mash the potatoes with the squash, butter and milk until smooth. Keep hot if serving now.

4. Steam the fish for 5 minutes until it is tender and flakes easily. Slide the salmon off the sticks before serving.

5. Serve with just cooked broccoli.

TIPS

- Freeze raw, wrapped in individual portions. Freeze the cooled mash in separate portions.

- As the fish is frozen raw on skewers, make sure to buy fish that hasn't already been frozen first.

- Always *remove* the skewers before serving and *never* leave children unattended while eating.

Mixed vegetable frittata

Makes enough for baby and you

Note: Not suitable for freezing

- 2 tsp **sunflower oil**
- 150g (5oz) cooked **potato**, diced
- 4 tbsp frozen **mixed vegetables**
- 3 **eggs**, beaten
- 1 tbsp freshly grated **Parmesan cheese**
- 1 tbsp organic **full-fat milk**
- 15g (½oz) unsalted **butter**

1. Heat the oil in a small frying pan, add the potato and fry for 4–5 minutes or until golden. Add the frozen vegetables and cook for 2–3 minutes or until softened.

2. Beat the eggs and cheese together with milk. Add the butter to the pan. When melted pour the egg mixture over the vegetables and cook for 3–4 minutes or until the omelette is set and the underside is golden.

3. Pre-heat the grill to high and cook the top of the omelette for 2–3 minutes until it is golden and the egg mixture is set all the way through. Leave to cool slightly then cut into wedges and serve with cherry tomatoes and cucumber.

TIPS

- This makes a speedy store cupboard supper and is ideal for when you've been out for the day. Perfect for a hungry toddler and his mum.

- Cold frittata also makes good picnic food served in mini pitta breads.

- Eggs are a very concentrated source of cheap protein and are perfectly safe for children as long as they are well cooked.

Chicken-peach casserole

Makes 6–8 servings

- 2 skinless, boneless **chicken breast fillets**, cubed
- 1 tbsp unsalted **butter**
- 1 tbsp **olive oil**
- 1 small **onion**, peeled and chopped
- 2 small **carrots**, peeled and diced
- 1 small **green pepper**, seeded and chopped
- 8 **cherry tomatoes**, halved
- 150ml (¼ pint) home-made **chicken** or **vegetable stock** (page 46) or filtered **water**
- 213g (7½oz) can sliced **peaches** in natural juice

1. Wash the chicken breasts under cold running water and dry with kitchen towel.

2. Heat the butter and oil in a large frying pan, add the chicken and fry for 3–4 minutes or until brown. Transfer the chicken pieces to a casserole dish.

3. Sweat the onion, carrots and green pepper in the remainder of the oil and butter for approximately 7–8 minutes, then add the tomato halves and the stock, and bring to the boil. Pour the peaches and juice or extra stock or water over the chicken pieces. Cover the casserole and cook for 30 minutes.

4. Serve mashed or finely chopped with rice or pasta.

TIPS

- Rather than canned fruit, use 125g (4oz) ready-to-eat peaches, cut into strips and an extra 150ml (¼ pint) water or stock.

- Serve with easy-cook brown rice or tiny soup pasta for extra texture.

Chinese noodles

Makes enough for baby and you

Note: Not suitable for freezing

- 65g (2½oz) **Chinese egg noodles**
- 2 tsp **sunflower oil**
- 1 small **carrot**, peeled and cut into thin strips
- ¼ **red pepper**, de-seeded and cut into strips
- 40g (1½oz) **green beans**, halved lengthways
- 50g (2oz) **pak choi**, well-rinsed and thinly sliced
- 1 cm (½in) piece **root ginger**, peeled and coarsely grated
- 1 tbsp **tomato ketchup**
- 4 tbsp boiling filtered **water**

1. Put the noodles into a shallow bowl, cover with boiling water and leave to soak or boil according to packet instructions.
2. Heat the oil in a wok or frying pan, add the carrot, red pepper and green bean strips and stir-fry for 3 minutes. Add the pak choi, ginger, ketchup and water and stir-fry for 2 minutes. Add the drained noodles, heat through and serve.

TIPS

- Delicious served topped with a thin egg omelette, rolled up like a Swiss roll and cut into thin strips.
- Beansprouts can be used in place of the pak choi.

Chicken with sweet peppers

Makes 2–3 servings

- 1 tbsp **olive oil**
- ¼ small **red onion**, finely sliced
- ½ **garlic** clove, crushed
- 1 **chicken breast fillet**, skinned, boned and cubed
- 200g (7oz) can chopped **tomatoes**
- ½ **red pepper**, chopped
- pinch of **mixed dried herbs** or 2 tsp finely chopped **fresh herbs**

1. Heat the oil in a saucepan, add the onion and crushed garlic, and sweat for 2–3 minutes.
2. Add the cubed chicken breast and fry in the oil for 1–2 minutes or until browned all over.
3. Add the tomatoes, peppers and herbs. Bring to the boil, then lower the heat and simmer, uncovered, for approximately 10–15 minutes.
4. Serve with rice or pasta.

TIPS

- Diced courgettes or mushrooms, or both, could also be added in place of the peppers.
- As your baby progresses to lumpier, coarser textures you may also like to serve this with soaked couscous or tiny cooked soup pasta.

Chicken and butter bean burgers

Makes 4 servings

Note: Only the burgers can be frozen

- 175g (6oz) minced **chicken**
- 100g (3½oz) canned **butter beans** (without salt or sugar) or **home-cooked beans**, drained
- 2 **spring onions**, roughly chopped
- **plain flour**, for shaping

To serve:

- 4 small soft **bread rolls**
- a little **tomato ketchup**
- a little shredded **lettuce**
- 1 **tomato**, thinly sliced

1. Put the chicken, beans and spring onions into a blender or food processor and blend together.
2. Shape into four small rounds with wet or floured hands. Wrap each burger in cling film, if freezing.
3. Pre-heat the grill to high. Cook burgers for 8 minutes, turning once or twice until they are browned and cooked through and the juices run clear when pierced with a knife. Cut one of the burgers in half, to make doubly sure they are cooked before serving.
4. Split the bread rolls, toast if liked and then spread one side with ketchup, add lettuce and tomato and top with a hot burger.

TIPS

- If your local supermarket doesn't sell ready-minced chicken, then buy the same weight of boneless, skinless chicken breast fillets and finely chop in a blender or food processor.

- For children who are not salad fans, leave the tomato and lettuce out of the bun and serve with carrot and cucumber sticks or slices of apple instead.

- Mixing the chicken with butter beans is a good way of introducing vegetable protein and fibre into your child's diet.

Chicken and mushroom stir-fry

Makes 2–3 servings

- 1 **chicken breast fillet**, skinned and boned
- 1 tsp **plain flour**
- 1 tsp **low-salt soy sauce**
- 2 tsp **vegetable oil**
- ¼ small **onion**, finely sliced
- ½ **garlic** clove, crushed
- 25g (1oz) **button mushrooms**, chopped

1. Cube the chicken into bite-sized pieces. Place in a bowl and coat with the flour, sprinkle with the soy sauce and leave for 15 minutes.

2. Heat the oil in wok or frying pan, add the chicken and stir-fry for 2–3 minutes. Lower the heat and push the chicken to one side, then add the onion and crushed garlic, if using. Cook for a further 2–3 minutes. Finally, mix in the mushrooms and stir-fry for a further 1–2 minutes.

3. Serve with pasta or rice.

TIPS

- Look out for low salt versions of soy sauce if you can.

- Vary the vegetables depending on what you have in the salad drawer, add strips of carrot, courgette, green bean, mangetout or red pepper if available.

Beef and barley pot supper

Makes 4–6 servings

- 300g (10oz) lean **minced beef**
- 1 small **onion**, finely chopped
- 2 tsp **olive oil**
- 225g (8oz) **carrot**, peeled and diced
- 150g (5oz) **swede**, peeled and diced
- 75g (3oz) **pearl (or pot) barley**, rinsed
- 900ml (1½ pints) home-made **chicken** or **vegetable stock** (page 46) or filtered **water**
- 1 tbsp **tomato purée**
- 1 **bouquet garni**, fresh or dried

1. Preheat the oven to 180°C/350°F/gas mark 4.
2. Fry the mince and onion in oil in a flameproof casserole or frying pan, stirring until browned.
3. Add the remaining ingredients and bring to the boil, stirring. Transfer to a casserole dish if not using a flameproof casserole dish. Cover and cook for 1½ hours or until the barley and vegetables are tender.
4. Remove the bouquet garni. Finely chop or mash the beef and barley as needed.

TIPS

- This mixture can also be spooned into individual ovenproof dishes and topped with mashed potato, shepherd's pie style.
- For adventurous babies add a little crushed garlic.

Chicken and vegetable oat crumble

Makes 4–6 servings

- 2 tbsp **olive oil**
- 2 **chicken breast fillets**, skinned and boned
- ½ small **onion**, diced
- 1 tbsp **plain flour**
- 300ml home-made **chicken** or **vegetable stock** (page 46) or filtered **water**
- 200g (7oz) **carrots**, diced
- 200g (7oz) **swede**, diced
- 100g (3½oz) **courgettes**, diced
- 2 sticks **celery**, diced

Topping:

- 5 tbsp fresh **wholemeal breadcrumbs**
- 5 tbsp **porridge oats**
- 5 tbsp grated mild **Cheddar cheese**

1. Preheat the oven to 200°C/400°F/gas mark 6
2. Heat the oil in a large saucepan, add the chicken and onion and fry until the chicken is sealed. Add the flour and cook for 1–2 minutes.
3. Gradually stir in the stock and cook over a low heat until it begins to thicken, then stir in the vegetables. Bring to the boil, then cover, lower the heat and simmer for 10–15 minutes or until the vegetables are just tender.
4. Meanwhile, mix together the topping ingredients and set aside.
5. Spoon the chicken and vegetable mixture into an ovenproof dish. Sprinkle over the topping ingredients and bake for 20–25 minutes or until the top is golden brown.
6. Serve mashed or finely chopped.

TIPS

- Adding a crunchy gratin-style topping is a good way to introduce texture to your baby's meals.

- If your child is naturally cutting down on milk, it can be helpful to know that just 40g (1½oz) of Cheddar cheese is equivalent to 200ml (7floz) of full-fat milk.

Kiddies' kedgeree

Makes 4 servings

- 2 tsp **olive oil**
- 1 small **onion**, finely chopped
- 100g (3½oz) **easy-cook long grain brown rice**, rinsed
- a large pinch of **ground turmeric**
- ¼ tsp **garam masala**
- 750ml (1¼ pints) home-made **vegetable stock** (page 46) or filtered **water**
- 2 **eggs**
- 75g (3oz) frozen **mixed vegetables**
- 200g (7oz) can **tuna** in spring water, well-drained and flaked

1. Heat the oil in a saucepan, add the onion and fry for 5 minutes or until soft. Stir in the rice and spices and cook for 1 minute.

2. Pour on the stock, bring to the boil, then cover, lower the heat and simmer for 30 minutes or until the rice is tender .

3. Meanwhile, put the eggs in a small saucepan and cover with cold water. Bring to the boil, cover, then lower the heat and simmer for 8 minutes or until hard-boiled. Drain. Peel the eggs and chop finely.

4. Add the vegetables, tuna and eggs to the rice. Spoon into the dishes, coarsely mashing or finely chopping to suit your baby.

TIPS

- Hard-boiled egg freezes well if very finely chopped.

- Brown rice contains more vitamins and minerals than white, but the phytic acid in the bran inhibits the absorption of iron and calcium. Easy-cook brown rice has some of the bran removed, making it a better alternative for young children.

Baby Bolognese
Makes 4–6 servings

- 150g (5oz) extra lean **minced beef steak**
- 1 small **onion**, peeled and finely chopped
- 75g (3oz) **button mushrooms**, wiped and sliced
- 200g (7oz) **carrots**, peeled and diced
- 150g (5oz) **courgettes**, diced
- a few stems of fresh **marjoram** or large pinch of dried marjoram
- **oil** for frying
- 600ml (1 pint) home-made **chicken stock** (page 46) or boiling filtered **water**
- 75g (3oz) **soup pasta**
- 2 tsp **tomato purée** (optional)

1. Dry-fry the meat and onion together in a saucepan until browned. Stir-fry the other vegetables with a little oil. Remove from the heat and add the herbs and stock or water. Return to the heat, cover and bring to the boil, then lower the heat and simmer for 30 minutes, stirring occasionally, until beef and vegetables are tender.

2. Meanwhile, cook pasta in a saucepan of boiling water for 6–7 minutes (or according to the packet instructions) or until tender. Drain well.

3. Purée the beef and pasta together in a blender, in batches if necessary. Mix in the tomato purée, if using.

TIPS

- As beef has a strong taste, use slightly less than other meats until your baby is happy with this new flavour.
- When your baby is older, adapt this dinner by puréeing the meat mixture and mixing with chopped pasta to introduce him to coarser, more textured dishes.

Pick-up sticks

Makes enough for baby and you

Note: Not suitable for freezing

- 1 small ripe **avocado**
- juice of ½ **lime**
- 1 tbsp organic **full-fat milk**
- 1 tsp chopped fresh **coriander leaves** (optional)
- 2 **pitta breads**
- selection **carrot**, **cucumber** and **celery** sticks

1. Mash the avocado with the lime juice and milk, add coriander, if using, and spoon the mixture into two small plastic dishes.
2. Pre-heat the grill to high. Sprinkle pitta bread with water and grill for 2–3 minutes. Leave to cool, then cut into strips and serve with veggy sticks and pots of avocado mixture.

TIPS

- Avocados are a powerhouse of concentrated energy – ideal for busy toddlers with small appetites.
- This kind of food is not only quick and easy to prepare but good to share with adults too.

5 Twelve Months and Over

By the age of 12 months your baby should be eating three meals a day and drinking all or most of his milk feeds from a beaker. He now needs a minimum of 350ml (12oz) a day and a maximum of 600ml (20oz), divided between two and three milk feeds and inclusive of milk used in cereal and cooking. Failure to discard the bottle after one year can lead many babies to drink well in excess of their daily requirements, which can make them very fussy about eating solids, and may even cause iron deficiency anaemia, as cow's milk is low in iron.

During the second year a child's growth slows down and there is often a decrease in appetite. I have quoted Elizabeth Morse, author of *My Child Won't Eat,* to hundreds of anxious parents who are worried about their child's eating habits. She says, 'If a child continued to grow at the same rate as in the first year, he would be 29 metres long and weigh 200 tonnes by the age of ten.' In my experience parents are often not made aware of this fact, and are unrealistic as to what their child really needs for a healthy and well-balanced diet during the second year. Constant pressure on the child to eat can lead to meal-times becoming a real battle of wills, creating long-term feeding problems.

If your baby does become very fussy during his second year and you are concerned that he is developing a feeding problem it might be a good idea to keep a food diary for at least one week. Some toddlers will eat very little for two or three days, then eat an enormous amount the following day. Refer to pages 4–8 on what your baby needs to eat for a healthy and well-balanced diet. For example, he needs three to four servings of carbohydrates a day, made up of cereal, bread, pasta or potatoes. It is very possible that your food diary will show a pattern where he is only eating one or two servings some days but has five or six on other days. This is perfectly normal and it is important to look at your child's food intake over several days, not the amount he eats in a single day. I have not included a feeding plan or recipes in this section, because once your baby is over a year old he should be eating a wide and varied range of meals, joining in most, if not all, of the family meals. Always remember, though, not to add salt until the baby's portion has been served.

The following guidelines should help you establish good eating habits for your toddler and hopefully help you to avoid serious eating problems.

Feeding guidelines

- If you wish to prevent your baby becoming a fussy feeder and a toddler who refuses healthy food, it is important to continue structuring his milk feeding so that the problem of excessive milk intake does not occur. He needs a minimum of 350ml (12oz) a day, divided between two and three milk feeds and inclusive of milk used in cooking and on cereal.

- Some toddlers will actually start to refuse their milk during the second year. If your toddler is taking less than the required minimum, try to increase the amount used on cereals and in sauces and healthy puddings. Include additional servings of yoghurt, fromage frais, cheese and dark green leafy vegetables, which are high in calcium.

- Good eating habits can be encouraged at this stage by introducing a wide variety of different tastes and textures and varying the way you prepare and serve his meals. Offer small quantities of different foods rather than large amounts of one or two foods. As your baby becomes more aware of different colours and shapes, try to make food look attractive. A selection of two or three different-coloured vegetables served with his chicken or fish at lunchtime will be much more appealing than the different foods still being mixed up altogether.

• Fruit juice can also take the edge off a toddler's appetite. Try to encourage water in between meals; if fruit juice is given it should be very well-diluted and offered no later than 2 hours before his meal. At mealtimes it is best to give your toddler at least half his food before offering water or juice – allowing drinks just before a meal may really affect his appetite.

• Look at the times you are feeding your toddler – an over-tired or over-hungry child will not eat well. Try to ensure that breakfast is finished by 8am, so that he is ready for lunch around 12 noon. This should ensure that he is ready for a good tea at 5pm.

• Avoid giving snacks or drinks too close to meal-times as they can take the edge off his appetite. Try to give mid-morning snacks and drinks around 9.30/10am and mid-afternoon snacks and drinks no later than 3pm.

• Try to stick to regular mealtimes and avoid distractions such as television or playing games. Avoid cajoling, forcing or bribing your toddler with puddings or sweets as an incentive to eat as this is one of the surest ways of creating a long-term eating problem. If your child starts to mess around with his food or become fussy, remove the food without making any comment about him not eating. Try then to make him wait until his next scheduled meal or snack before giving him anything to eat or drink.

• Sugar is another cause of loss of appetite and levels can be quite high in many commercial foods such as baked beans, tinned soups, fruits, etc. Some leading brands of fromage frais have as much as 14.5g of sugar in a 100g pot. Always check the label for the list of ingredients and avoid food with high levels of sugar, starches and fillers, all of which can reduce a toddler's appetite for healthy food.

• Most babies can eat the same foods as the rest of the family as long as they are cut into bite-sized pieces. Encouraging your baby to self-feed at this stage also plays a very important part in establishing good feeding habits. Try to avoid being over-fussy about how messy meals have become. The important thing is that your baby feels happy and relaxed at mealtimes and is attempting to get the food into his mouth, even if it is mostly by using his fingers.

Davina: aged 18 months

Davina first started to refuse milk when she was 14 months old. By the time she was 18 months old she was drinking no milk at all, although she would take milk on her breakfast cereal. Davina's parents sought medical advice from both the health visitor and local GP. They were advised to give her lots of cheese and yoghurt, as well as milk on cereal, to compensate for her refusal to drink milk. The reason they contacted me was that they were very worried about Davina's other fluid intake, which amounted to approximately 180–240ml (6–8oz) a day. They were also worried about the fact that she was still eating jars of baby food, was eating a very limited range of foods and that each meal was becoming a battle of wills, with her refusing to be spoon-fed. They would dance, sing and cajole her into eating, often resorting to force-feeding her.

I advised Davina's parents to keep a very detailed food diary of everything she ate and drank, also the exact amounts consumed and the times she ate. Once I received this it was clear that much of the problem was being caused by her snacks in between meals and the jars of food. Davina's food diary consisted of the following:

Breakfast: 8.20am

1 Weetabix with milk and chopped fruit

3 mini bix

¼ slice of toast with butter and Marmite

60 ml (2oz) water

Lunch: 12.40pm

1 large jar of organic baby food, eaten with great reluctance

1 large yoghurt

½ slice of bread and butter

1 dessertspoon of flaked fish

½ Baby Bel cheese

30ml (1oz) water

3.30pm

1 slice of ginger cake

½ slice of bread and butter

Tea: 6pm

1 large jar of organic baby food

1 large yoghurt

1 tablespoon of peas and sweetcorn

1 tablespoon of mixed bean salad

1 slice cucumber

¼ croissant

60ml (2oz) water

3 mini bix

As Davina was becoming very difficult about eating from the spoon, I advised her parents to cut out her mini bix and reduce her amount of Weetabix in the morning so that she took all her yoghurt and fruit requirements first thing in the morning when she was really hungry. This had the knock-on effect of making her hungrier at lunchtime. We stopped the jars altogether and offered her a selection of cold cuts of very thinly sliced meats or fish, and finger food vegetables at lunchtime so that she could be in control of her feeding. Within two days she was actually taking all her protein and vegetable requirements at lunch so that we could be more relaxed about tea. We stopped giving her cake and bread mid-afternoon and replaced it with a small piece of fresh fruit, which made her hungry for her tea. Then at teatime we offered her a selection of finger food vegetables and salad, with cheese and bread, followed by either carrot or banana cake. By the end of the week her food diary showed that all her food requirements were being met and, even better, she trebled her fluid intake.

Your questions answered

Q My toddler's eating habits have become very erratic over the last few months. Some days he will eat three good meals a day, on other days just one, and some days he just snacks all day. How do I get him back to eating three good meals a day?

A • This erratic eating pattern is very common during a child's second and third year and, as long as he is eating healthy food, it is better to go with it. In my experience children who are cajoled, bribed or forced to eat usually end up with long-term eating problems. However, it is important to set some rules and boundaries about eating to ensure that your child's nutritional needs are met with a variety of healthy foods over a period of several days.

• Allow a certain length of time for meals. If your child is fussing and refusing food after this time, don't make any comment, simply remove the meal and make him wait for any further food until his next snack or meal is due.

• Keep a food diary, listing all the foods and drinks your child consumes and at what times. Make a note of his behaviour at mealtimes and whether you think his lack of appetite could have been caused by over-tiredness or getting over-excited.

• Pay very close attention to the timing and type of snacks you are giving. Snacks and drinks should always be given midway between meals – giving them too close to a meal can take the edge off a toddler's appetite. It is also important to select healthy snacks that are not too filling – fresh and dried fruit or raw chopped vegetables are preferable to more filling foods such as cheese, bread sticks or biscuits. Try to avoid things like sweets, ice-creams and crisps as they are of little nutritional value and will fill your toddler up with empty calories.

• Excessive milk intake is another cause of toddlers not eating well at mealtimes. Your toddler needs a minimum of 350ml (12oz) and a maximum of 600ml (20oz) of full-fat milk a day. These amounts are best given as a drink first thing in the morning and on breakfast cereal and as a drink last thing at night, with the remainder used in cooking. Milk given as a drink between meals can really take the edge off the appetite.

Q **My toddler is eating a wide variety of carbohydrates, such as bread, pasta and potatoes, plus lots of fruit and**

vegetables, as finger foods, but I am having real problems getting him to eat meat or fish.

A • Many toddlers do refuse to eat meat at this age. Try offering very thinly cut slices of chicken, turkey, lamb or beef spread with a little Marmite. Good-quality meat or vegetarian sausages are also worth trying. The important thing is not to force your toddler to eat something he clearly dislikes. There are many vegetarian alternatives that can provide him with all his protein needs.

• Offering your toddler plenty of pulses or legumes e.g. soya, lentils and chick peas, cheese, yoghurt, soya and eggs with his other foods will ensure that he receives enough protein. It is also worthwhile investing in a couple of recipe books that specialise in vegetarian cookery for children to make sure you fully understand how to combine vegetable proteins so that your baby receives a nutritionally balanced diet.

Q **My toddler has suddenly taken a real dislike to his milk and is now taking a lot less than 350ml (12oz) a day. Some nights he flatly refuses his bedtime drink.**

A • Babies and young toddlers are not capable of distinguishing the difference between hunger and thirst, therefore it would be wise to check that your toddler is not eating too much solid food at mealtimes, which could have a knock-on effect on the amount of milk he is drinking. For several days keep a note of all the food, milk and other fluids that he consumes over each 24-hour period and the times he consumes them. Check on pages 122–4 for guidelines on how much a toddler needs to eat at this age. If the amounts he is eating over several days seem well in excess of the guidelines, gradually cut back on his solids to see if this helps increase the amount of milk he wants.

- When toddlers refuse milk at this age it is sometimes because they have drunk too much water or juice in the late afternoon, which then affects their bedtime bottle. Try to offer your child a mid-afternoon drink of water only no later than 3pm, and offer only a couple of ounces of fluids with his tea.

- Record details of the times he does drink milk and the amounts he consumes. Gradually reduce his milk intake during the day to see if he will increase the amount he takes at bedtime.

- If your toddler still refuses his milk offer him a yoghurt at both breakfast and lunch, and include a serving of cheese in his daily diet. Also try to include lots of sauces and milk puddings in his diet and milk-shake drinks made with fruit and fromage frais or yoghurt.

6 A-Z of Foods

Apples (from four months)

Apples are an ideal first weaning food but need to be cooked and puréed until your baby reaches six months of age. They can then be given raw, but should still be peeled and puréed or grated. Between nine and twelve months, the majority of babies are able to chew small pieces of soft peeled apple.

Health benefits

Apples are reported to help reduce cholesterol levels and contain cancer-fighting agents. They are high in soluble fibre, which can help prevent constipation when eaten raw. They are also a good source of vitamin C and bioflavonoids. Note that the vitamin C content varies considerably, depending on the variety of apple.

Buying and storing

Choose eating apples that are firm, brightly coloured and without blemishes. To keep them moist and crisp, remove any plastic wrapping and store the fruit at a cool temperature or in the refrigerator.

Preparation

To prevent the apple turning brown do not peel or slice it until you are ready to cook it. It should then be peeled, quartered, cored, covered with a small amount of freshly filtered water, and cooked as soon as possible.

Cooking

Add just enough freshly filtered boiling water to cover, then put a lid on the pan, lower the heat and simmer until soft. Remove the apple from the water and purée to a smooth texture in a blender, adding some of the cooking liquid to get the desired consistency. When cool, the required amount should be given to your baby immediately, and any leftovers put in a suitable container and stored in the refrigerator.

Apricots (from six months)

Fresh apricots are best introduced at around six months, when they can be given raw. Dried apricots can also be given from six months onwards, but would need to be cooked and puréed until your baby is around one year old and able to chew them properly.

Health benefits

Fresh and dried apricots are very rich in anti-oxidants, particularly beta-carotene. Dried apricots, in particular, are an excellent source of iron, are high in fibre and a good source of potassium. They are said to offer some protection against cancer and respiratory infections, and may help to regulate blood pressure.

Buying and storing

Choose fresh apricots with firm smooth skins that are blemish-free. Hard, under-ripe fruits should be avoided, as they tend to have a sour taste. Apricots should be stored in the refrigerator and used within two to three days.

Preparation

Although fresh apricots can be served raw, either mashed or puréed, from six months it is advisable to remove the skins. Wash them in a colander under cold running water, then cover with filtered, boiled water for approximately one minute, then for one minute with cold water to loosen the skins. Peel away the skins, and cut the fruits in quarters to remove the stone and pith. Purée to a smooth texture using a blender or mash finely with a fork. If necessary a small amount of cool, freshly filtered boiled water can be used to get the desired consistency. Dried stoneless apricots should be washed in a colander under cold running water and placed in a pan with enough fresh filtered water to cover.

Cooking

Bring the fruit to the boil, cover with a lid and simmer until tender. Drain the fruit and purée to a smooth texture in a blender. If necessary use the reserved liquid to adjust the purée to the desired consistency.

Asparagus (from six to seven months)

Asparagus can be introduced in cooking from six to seven months, but it is best used as a finger food when your baby is getting towards a year old.

Health benefits

Asparagus is an excellent source of the antioxidants glutathione and beta carotene, which may help to prevent certain cancers. It is also a good source of the vitamins A and C. Asparagus is also reported to have sedative qualities and can act as a mild diuretic.

Buying and storing

Choose firm and fresh looking stalks. Whether they are green or white depends on the variety rather than the quality, but avoid any that look droopy or have thin, wrinkled or woody stems. Since asparagus needs to be eaten really fresh, the further it has travelled, the less likely it is to be the best quality. Asparagus should be kept in the bottom of the fridge with other perishable vegetables

Preparation

Rinse each stalk gently and break or cut off the end if it is tough and woody. Scrape or shave the lengths of each stalk, starting just below the tip. Trim the stalks to roughly the same lengths and then tie them in bundles of six to eight stalks for steaming, tying them under the tips and near the base of the stalks.

Cooking

Wedge the bundles, tips facing upwards in a deep saucepan with enough filtered boiling water to come three quarters of the way up the stalks. Cover the tips with a cap of foil and simmer gently until tender. This means the stalks are boiled and the delicate tips are steamed. Very fresh asparagus will need to cook for only three to five minutes, otherwise for about ten minutes. Drain well on kitchen towel and freshen under cold water, then drain and serve either mashed or chopped.

Aubergine (from nine to twelve months)

This can be popular when stuffed with layers of cheese and tomato and then roasted. It is a great vegetable to add to dishes like moussaka.

Health benefits

Aubergines are not reported to have any particular health benefits, apart from being low in fat and sodium. They contain a small amount of the vitamin B_2 and medium amounts of vitamin B_1 and potassium.

Buying and storing

Choose firm, smooth aubergines with dark shiny blemish-free skins. Aubergines can be kept for five to seven days if refrigerated.

Preparation

To prevent aubergines turning brown they should not be cut until they are ready to be cooked. Wash under cold running water and dry with kitchen towel.

Cooking

Aubergines are best used in dishes such as moussaka and other savoury bakes.

Avocado (from five to six months)

Avocado is often recommended as a first weaning food. However, because of its high fat content I prefer to wait until five to six months before introducing it. I have found that many babies take longer to digest it than other first weaning foods, causing them to cut back too much on the following milk feed.

Health benefits

Avocado is an excellent source of vitamin E, and provides reasonable amounts of vitamins A, B and C. It is also a good source of potassium and protein. It has a high level of monounsaturated fat which is believed to help lower blood cholesterol levels, and some experts believe it can also help prevent clogging of the arteries.

Buying and storing

Choose avocados with smooth, shiny bright green blemish-free skins, as they tend to be sweeter than the dark green or purple-coloured ones. The avocado is ripe if the ends of fruit feel soft when pressed. Ripe avocados are best stored at a cool temperature or in the refrigerator, where they should keep for three to four days. Avocados cannot be frozen.

Preparation

Wash under cold running water, cut in half and remove the stone. Scoop the flesh from one half and mash to a smooth texture using a fork. If necessary the consistency can be adjusted by mixing in a small amount of formula, expressed milk or cool freshly boiled water. The remaining half of the fruit should be brushed with lemon juice and wrapped tightly in foil and stored immediately in the refrigerator.

Cooking

Avocados require no cooking and are best served in salads or mashed as dips.

Bananas (from five to six months)

Highly recommended as a first weaning food, and can be introduced at four months. However, I prefer to introduce them later because I have found that bananas mixed with baby rice can cause constipation and digestive problems for many babies under six months old.

Health benefits

Bananas are high in the mineral potassium, which is essential for good muscle and nerve function and regulating blood pressure. They are also said to be effective in treating stomach upsets and diarrhoea, especially when served with rice and cooked apples. Because bananas are very high in natural sugars, they are believed to be very effective in raising energy levels.

Buying and storing

Choose creamy yellow-coloured bananas with smooth blemish-free skins. Allow two or three days for them to ripen; once they have developed brown spots on their skins they are ready to eat. If the fruit has touches of green on it, it will need longer to ripen and should not be used as it can cause severe indigestion in young babies. Bananas should be stored at room temperature, not in the refrigerator. Bananas cannot be frozen.

Preparation

Bananas require no cooking and should not be cut or peeled until they are ready to be eaten as they very quickly turn brown. When required, peel and mash half a banana to a smooth texture with a fork, using formula, breast milk or cool, freshly boiled water.

Barley (from five to six months)

Choose barley in plastic or cellophane packs so that you can see it is clean, free from stones and other rubbish, and that it is not mouldy. Pot barley contains more micronutrients than pearl barley because it includes the husk, but babies find it harder to chew.

Health benefits

Barley is a high carbohydrate food which is a good source of the B vitamins and reputed to be very beneficial in providing energy and keeping blood sugar levels steady. It is also believed to reduce cholesterol levels and help fight heart disease.

Buying and storing

Store in an airtight container in a cool, dark place. Barley keeps well, but after six months the skin begins to toughen and takes an increasingly longer time to cook, so buy it from a supplier with a fast turnover of stock.

Preparation

Pick over the barley and discard any damaged or darkened grains.

Cooking

Place in a large saucepan and cover with filtered cold water. Bring to the boil, drain and rinse with filtered cold water. Return to a saucepan and cover in filtered cold water. Bring to the boil, lower the heat, simmer for 1¼ hours or until tender. Drain well.

Beans see **Green beans** and **Pulses**

Beansprouts (from one year)

These can be a great finger food to give alongside any dish, but are best served in a salad.

Health benefits

Beansprouts are not renowned for having any particular health benefits but they are a good source of vitamin C, and provide medium amounts of the B vitamins and the mineral potassium.

Buying and storing

Choose crisp, small, fresh shoots or grow them yourself at home. Beansprouts take only four to seven days to sprout from mung beans. Beansprouts should be kept in the bottom of the fridge with other salad and perishable vegetables.

Preparation

Rinse in filtered water.

Cooking

Cook as soon as possible after buying or harvesting. Either blanch for 30 seconds in filtered boiling water or stir-fry for one to two minutes. Serve hot as an accompaniment, cold as part of a salad or stir-fried with other vegetable ingredients and meat or chicken.

Beef (from nine to twelve months)

Although the COMA guidelines say that beef can be introduced at four to six months, I have found that it is best introduced when your baby is able to eat mince without it being puréed. I always find that a simple cottage pie or lasagne is popular.

Health benefits

Beef is high in protein and an excellent source of vitamins and minerals, particularly the B vitamins and iron and zinc.

Buying and storing

Choose good-quality organic beef – the leanest cuts are rump or fillet. It is important to remove beef from the plastic packaging it is bought in, particularly if it is not going to be cooked on the day of purchase. All beef should be washed under cold running water, and dried with kitchen towel before being stored in the coldest part of the refrigerator. Once cleaned, it should be placed on a clean plate and loosely covered with foil.

It is very important to keep raw meat separate from cooked meat. Store raw meat in the coldest part of the refrigerator.

Preparation
Trim the beef carefully, cutting away all the visible fat.

Cooking
Less tender cuts need added liquid and longer slower cooking; methods here include braising, pot roasting, stewing and boiling. The tender cuts of meat are best cooked quickly by dry heat, either roasting, grilling or dry-frying.

Beetroot (from nine to twelve months)
Although it is possible to purée beetroot, I have never found it to be very popular with babies, and usually wait until the baby is taking mashed or diced food before introducing it.

Health benefits
Beetroot is an excellent source of potassium and folic acid. It is also believed to offer protection against some cancers.

Buying and storing
Choose small, firm smooth beets with blemish-free skins. Like potatoes and turnips they are best stored in a cool dark airy cupboard, where they should keep for about two months. If stored at room temperature they would need to be used within a week.

Preparation
Wash the beets under cold running water, taking care not to break the skin. Trim slightly the tops and roots.

Cooking

Put the beets in a large pan with plenty of freshly filtered water. Bring to the boil, cover and simmer until tender. Drain and carefully remove the skins by rubbing. They can then be mashed or diced as and when needed. Any remaining beets can be stored in the refrigerator.

Berries (from nine to twelve months)

Although blackberries, blackcurrants, blueberries, cranberries, etc., can be introduced sooner than nine months in a purée, they are so fiddly to prepare that I usually wait until the baby is well established on finger foods, and introduce them raw at that stage.

Health benefits

All berries are a good source of vitamin C and can help improve iron absorption when eaten alongside non-meat sources of iron, e.g. breakfast cereals. However, they may cause allergies in children from allergic families, so should be introduced with care into the diet of such babies.

Buying and storing

Choose plump, fresh and firm-looking fruit that is stored in containers with no signs of leaking. Fruit that is leaking is potentially mouldy. Berries should be loosely covered in brown paper bags, kept in the refrigerator and used within two to three days.

Preparation

Wash the berries in a colander under cold running water. Remove stems and leaves and any crushed fruit. Check for grubs when doing this, particularly with fruit that already has stems missing.

Cooking

Berries can be given whole to babies over nine months old who have mastered eating several finger foods. For babies who are still learning to eat finger foods the berries should be puréed to a smooth texture then put through a sieve to remove the skins and seeds.

Bread (from six to seven months)

Once you are confident that your baby can tolerate wheat (in breakfast cereal and pasta) then you can introduce him to bread. The easiest way is first to introduce it as breadcrumbs used as a topping on vegetable or fish pies. As your baby's chewing develops and he shows signs of wanting to feed himself he will enjoy small bite-sized pieces of buttered toast, particularly when he starts teething.

Health benefits

Bread is a good source of carbohydrate and starch. Wholemeal bread has a higher fibre content than white, but all bread is a good source of B vitamins.

Buying and storing

Choose an organic wholemeal loaf which is free of whole grains of any sort. Bread is best stored in a separate bread bin where the air is able to circulate, and it should stay fresh for three to four days.

Preparation

Introduce bread as a topping on cooked dishes. Cut off the crusts and place the bread in a food processor for a few moments until it has turned to very fine breadcrumbs. Depending on the recipe, it can be mixed with a variety of different foods, such as cheese and oats to form a nutritious topping on vegetable bakes, fish pies and meat casseroles, etc.

Once your baby is capable of self-feeding he can be offered small pieces of toast with butter and miniature sandwiches with different spreads on. Breadsticks are also very popular with babies who are used to finger foods.

Broccoli (from six to seven months)

Once your baby is eating a variety of the different root vegetables and the blander green vegetables, you can try introducing broccoli. By starting off with very small amounts – say, one tablespoonful of broccoli mixed with two to three tablespoonfuls of sweet potato plus one to two tablespoonfuls of carrot, your baby will be less likely to reject the broccoli.

Health benefits

Broccoli is rich in antioxidants and believed to help protect against cancer, particularly cancer of the lungs and breast. It is a good source of vitamin C and contains useful amounts of potassium and folic acid.

Buying and storing

Choose dark-coloured, fresh-looking broccoli with firm stalks and tightly closed heads. It should be stored in the refrigerator and used within two to three days.

Preparation

Rinse under cold running water then soak in salted water for 30 minutes to get rid of any insects. Trim the stalks and remove the leaves and break into even-sized florets. It then needs to be washed several times under cold running water to remove the salt.

Cooking

Place florets in a pan and cover with cold filtered water. Bring to the boil, then lower the heat and simmer, uncovered, until tender. Remove from cooking liquid and purée to a smooth texture using a blender. Any remaining cooking liquid can be used to get the right consistency.

Brussels sprouts (from eight to nine months)

Brussels sprouts can cause quite severe wind in young babies so I rarely introduce them before eight months. If your baby is happy taking other green vegetables, such as cabbage or broccoli, with no side effects, now is the time to try Brussels sprouts.

Health benefits
Brussels sprouts are high in antioxidants and other cancer-fighting agents which may be of help in preventing cancer of the colon and stomach.

Buying and storing
Choose small, firm sprouts with fresh-looking and compact, brightly coloured green leaves. Store as for asparagus.

Preparation
The sprouts should be plunged into cold salted water to get rid of any bugs. They should then be trimmed and a cross cut in the base of the sprout. Finally, they should be washed thoroughly in a colander under cold running water.

Cooking
Put the sprouts in a pan and cover with just enough freshly filtered boiled water, then lower the heat and simmer, uncovered, until the sprouts are tender. Drain off the water, and either chop the sprouts roughly or cut into bite-sized pieces, depending on how well your baby is at chewing at this stage. A small knob of butter will enhance their flavour.

Butter (from six to seven months)

Initially I would only use small amounts of butter in cooking. Once finger foods are established it is excellent on bread or toast.

Health benefits

Butter is a good source of vitamins A and D. However, it is also high in saturated fat and calories, so use it in moderation.

Buying and storing

Use unsalted butter for children. Butter is also perfect for freezing for up to six months. Defrost thoroughly before using.

Preparation

When used for cooking, butter is a natural product and gives good flavour to baking. Store butter in the fridge or in a cool dark place, well wrapped or covered to prevent it from absorbing other flavours. Butter will keep for two to three weeks (or until the 'best before' date on the package).

Cooking

Remove butter from the fridge at least one hour before cooking to allow it to soften.

Cabbage (from seven to eight months)

Cabbage is another vegetable that can cause problems with wind in some babies. Your baby will be more likely to accept the cabbage if it is introduced in small amounts, and mixed with two to three tablespoonfuls of creamed potato.

When your baby is between nine and twelve months old and eating a wide variety of chopped and cubed food, you can try offering him a small amount of very finely chopped cabbage.

Health benefits

Cabbage is high in vitamin C and is believed to contain antioxidants that may help prevent cancer of the colon.

Buying and storing

Choose cabbages with tightly closed leaves that look fresh and crisp and feel heavy for their size. Cabbages should be stored loosely in a paper bag in the refrigerator and used within five to seven days.

Preparation
Wash cabbage leaves under a cold running tap and break into small pieces.

Cooking
Put the cabbage leaves in a pan and cover with a very small amount of filtered water. Bring to the boil, then lower the heat and simmer, uncovered, until tender. Remove from the cooking liquid and purée to a very smooth texture in a blender. Any remaining cooking liquid can be used to get the right consistency. Alternatively a knob of butter can be added.

Carrots (from four to five months)
Carrots are one of the most popular weaning foods, loved by the majority of babies. However, keep a watchful eye on the quantities you give and how often. It is important to give babies a balanced diet, and too much of any one food is undesirable.

Health benefits
Carrots are rich in beta carotene, the antioxidant believed to help fight numerous different types of cancers. They are also an excellent source of vitamin A, which helps maintain healthy vision.

Buying and storing
Choose firm, brightly coloured carrots with smooth unblemished skins. Store as for green beans.

Preparation
Wash under cold running water. Young, tender carrots can be scrubbed with a vegetable brush, but older ones will need to be scraped or peeled, then rinsed and sliced.

Cooking

Put carrots in a pan covered with freshly boiled filtered water, bring to the boil, then cover, lower the heat and simmer until tender. Remove from cooking liquid and purée to a smooth texture in a blender. Any remaining cooking liquid can be used to get the right consistency.

Cauliflower (from five to six months)

Cauliflower can be introduced once your baby is taking a variety of different vegetables. I find that most young babies prefer it mixed with a little formula or expressed milk or baby rice and served with one or two other vegetables.

Health benefits

Cauliflower is a good source of potassium and vitamin C, and is believed to protect against cancer.

Buying and storing

Choose cauliflowers with creamy white closely packed heads that have no brown spots, and have fresh-looking green leaves. Store as for green beans.

Preparation

Remove the outer green leaves and cut off the woody stem. Break the florets into even-sized pieces and wash well under cold running water.

Cooking

Put florets in a pan and cover with filtered water. Bring to the boil, then lower the heat and simmer, uncovered, until tender. Remove from the heat and purée to a smooth texture in a blender. Any remaining cooking liquid can be used to achieve the right consistency. Alternatively, use a small amount of formula or expressed milk.

Celery (from eight to nine months)

Although some recipe books do introduce celery as a purée, it is not something that I personally have found to be popular with very young babies. I usually introduce it cooked in soups, stews and casseroles from eight months.

Health benefits
Celery is believed to be high in compounds that may help to lower blood pressure and cholesterol levels.

Buying and storing
Choose crisp, light-coloured celery with fresh-looking leaves and blemish-free stalks – the darker green the celery the more stringy it will be. Celery should be stored, loosely wrapped, in the refrigerator and used within one week.

Preparation
Use the inner stalks for babies as they tend to be less tough. Cut off the roots of the stalks and the leaves. Wash well under cold running water, then slice or dice as required.

Cooking
Sauté finely chopped celery and use in stews and soups.

Cheese (from six to seven months)

Because cheese can trigger allergies in some allergic babies it is advisable to start off with very small amounts. It can be used in cooking and is a great finger food.

Health benefits
Cheddar cheese is an excellent source of protein and calcium and is the first cheese to be introduced. Cottage cheese and cream cheese are also high in protein but low in calcium, and some cream

cheeses can be very high in salt and should not be given to babies and young children. Choose low-salt varieties. Cheeses such as Camembert and Brie, etc., are not recommended for children under one yearof age.

Buying and storing
Choose a mild organic Cheddar cheese that is free from additives and preservatives. Cheese is best wrapped in greaseproof paper to stop it sweating.

Preparation
Finely grate for use in sauces and sandwiches, or cut into sticks.

Cooking
Mild Cheddar cheese can be served in sauces or mixed with vegetarian dishes from six months onwards.

Chicken see Poultry

Courgettes (from four to five months)
Courgettes are an ideal first green vegetable to introduce. In my experience very few babies dislike it, especially if it is mixed with sweet potato, baby rice or carrot.

Health benefits
Courgettes are a good source of beta carotene, vitamin C, potassium and folic acid.

Buying and storing
Choose small dark green courgettes with smooth blemish-free skins. Larger courgettes are more likely to have a slightly bitter taste. Store as for green beans.

Preparation
Wash courgettes under cold running water, cut off the ends and slice.

Cooking
Put in a pan and cover with cold filtered water, bring to the boil, then lower the heat and simmer, uncovered until tender. Remove from the cooking liquid and purée to a smooth texture using a blender. Any remaining cooking liquid can be used to achieve the right consistency.

Cucumber (from nine to twelve months)
Once your baby is managing to eat and chew a variety of finger foods well, you can introduce cucumber. Some babies find it more palatable if the skin is removed.

Health benefits
Cucumbers are a source of vitamin C and contain some potassium.

Buying and storing
Choose firm cucumbers with smooth green unblemished skins. Store them in the salad drawer of your refrigerator and use within one week.

Preparation
Wash the cucumber under cold running water, then chop, slice, or dice into sizes that you think your baby will manage to eat. If you prefer to peel the cucumber, do so just prior to giving it to your baby so that the vitamin C content is not destroyed.

Cooking
Cucumber does not need to be cooked and is best served with salads or dips.

Eggs (from eight to nine months)

Hard-boiled egg yolk can be introduced from eight months, and the hard-boiled white between nine and twelve months. After nine to twelve months, eggs can be scrambled or cooked as an omelette. Soft-boiled eggs should be avoided until your child is one year.

Health benefits

Eggs are an excellent source of vitamin B_{12} and protein and are rich in minerals. The yolks are also a good source of vitamins A and D, but they are high in fat and cholesterol.

Buying and storing

Choose organic free-range eggs and store them in the refrigerator well away from any powerful-smelling foods.

Preparation

Test for freshness just before cooking. Put the egg in a bowl of water; if it floats to the surface it is likely to be old and possibly bad, because the size of the natural air pocket in the egg increases in age. If it stays at the bottom it is fresh.

Cooking

Eggs can be hard-boiled, scrambled or cooked in an omelette.

Figs (from eight to nine months)

Figs are not the most popular food with young babies, but it is worthwhile trying them as they are very nutritious. Once your baby has tasted other dried fruits such as apricots and dates you could try introducing some chopped or puréed figs with breakfast cereal.

Health benefits

Figs are a good source of iron and potassium. Dried figs are also high in fibre, which can prevent constipation.

Buying and storing

There are green, white, purple and black varieties of fig. They have soft, creamy pink flesh full of tiny edible seeds. Most varieties have thin skins, which are edible, though some people prefer to peel figs before eating. Fresh figs should be soft to the touch. They do not keep well, so place in a fruit bowl and eat soon after purchase.

Preparation

Wash half a dozen figs in a colander under cold running water, then leave to soak in a bowl of freshly filtered water overnight.

Cooking

Rinse and put in a pan covered with freshly filtered water. Bring to the boil, cover with a lid, then lower the heat and simmer until the fruit is tender. Remove from the cooking liquid and either purée to a very smooth texture using a blender, or chop into small pieces using a sharp kitchen knife. Serve the figs with your baby's breakfast cereal, yoghurt, rice pudding or custard.

Fish (from six months)

Fish is very nutritious but should be avoided before six months because of the risk of allergies. White fish, such as cod, plaice and haddock, and oily fish, such as salmon and tuna, are equally acceptable. Shellfish can be introduced from 18 months.

Health benefits

Fish is an excellent source of protein and is high in omega-3 fatty acids, which are very healthy for our hearts. Fish is also a good source of vitamin B_{12}. Fish oils and fatty fish are good sources of vitamins A and D.

Buying and storing

Choose fillets of fish that look fresh and moist, have no fishy smell, and are completely free from bones. Fish should be washed under cold running water, then dried with kitchen towel. It should then be placed on a plate which is loosely covered with foil and stored in the coldest part of the refrigerator. All fresh fish should be cooked within 24 hours.

Preparation
Wash a small cod or haddock fillet (approx 50g/2 oz) and dry with kitchen towel. Place the fillet in a pan with just enough milk or filtered water to cover it.

Cooking
Bring cooking liquid to the boil, then lower the heat and simmer, uncovered, until tender. Remove the fish from the cooking liquid, check for bones then purée to a smooth texture using a blender. Any remaining cooking liquid can be used to achieve the right consistency. This fish purée should be mixed with a choice of two or three vegetable purées.

Garlic (from nine months)
Garlic can be used in very small amounts from nine months.

Health benefits
Garlic contains a substance that helps fight infections, and may even protect against viruses.

Buying and storing
Choose firm cloves with tight-clinging skin. Store in a cool dry place but not close to other foods as they will absorb the garlic's smell.

Preparation
To peel garlic easily, blanch the cloves in boiling water for about 30 seconds, then drain and cool. Slice off the root. To get the most garlicky taste from garlic cloves, chop or mash them or extract the oil with a garlic press.

Cooking
Garlic should be chopped finely and then lightly fried until soft.

Grapes (from nine to twelve months)
Grapes, like cherries, can be given earlier than nine months as a raw purée. But I usually wait until babies are finger feeding themselves and chewing well, which is usually between nine and twelve months.

Health benefits
Grapes are a good source of potassium. Black grapes are a good source of antioxidants, which help reduce heart disease.

Buying and storing
Choose firm, blemish-free seedless grapes that are still attached to their stems. Grapes are best stored loosely wrapped in the refrigerator and used within three to four days.

Preparation
Grapes should be washed just before eating in a colander under cold running water.

Cooking
Put six grapes in a blender and purée to a smooth texture, then press through a sieve to discard the skins. For babies over nine months who are chewing well, grapes can be chopped, mashed or given as halves.

Green beans (from four to five months)
French or runner beans are often refused by young babies, so it is important that, like broccoli, the bean purée in the early stages is mixed with enough sweet potato to get your baby gradually used to the taste.

Health benefits
Green beans are a good source of beta carotene, folate, vitamin C and potassium. Some beans are believed to be helpful in regulating blood sugar and cholesterol levels and preventing heart disease.

Buying and storing
Choose small firm crisp green beans, with unblemished, good-coloured skins. Green beans should be stored loosely wrapped in a paper bag in the refrigerator and used within five to six days.

Preparation
Wash beans in a colander under cold running water, then top and tail and remove any strings.

Cooking
Put the beans in a pan and just cover with cold filtered water. Bring to the boil then lower the heat and simmer, uncovered, until tender. Remove from the pan and purée to a smooth texture in a blender. Any remaining cooking liquid can be used to achieve the right consistency.

Lamb (from seven to eight months)
If your baby has had no problems digesting chicken, lamb would be the next meat to try. Introducing lamb in casseroles and shepherd's pie is popular with most babies. Note, however, that fatty cuts are high in saturated fats.

Health benefits
Whilst lamb is high in protein and a rich source of most B vitamins, iron, zinc, potassium and phosphorus, it has a higher proportion of saturated fatty acids and more cholesterol than poultry, pork and most beef cuts. Even, lean cuts of lamb should be chosen and trimmed of excess fat.

Buying and storing

Home-produced lamb is at its best in spring, but there is a good supply of imported lamb all year round. Shoulder and leg of lamb are now cut into steaks, and minced lamb is more widely available. When storing, wash, then dry with kitchen towel and store in the fridge loosely wrapped with kitchen foil.

Preparation

Trim off all fat.

Cooking

There are two basic ways of cooking lamb. Less tender cuts need added liquid and longer, slower cooking, such as braising, pot roasting, stewing and boiling. Tender cuts of meat are best cooked quickly by dry heat – roasting, grilling or dry-frying.

Lentils (from six to seven months)

Red lentils are a favourite with many babies, particularly when used in soups and casseroles. Lentils are classed as an incomplete protein and need to be served with other grains if they are to substitute animal protein as a complete protein. They can cause wind.

Health benefits

Lentils are high in vitamin B_6 (pyridoxine), folic acid, iron, potassium, selenium and manganese. They are also a good source of protein and fibre and may be of use to diabetics because they help to regulate blood sugar levels. They lower cholesterol levels, which assists in the fight against heart disease.

Buying and storing

Choose lentils that are well packed, smooth-skinned and evenly coloured. Once opened, lentils are best transferred to an airtight jar or container, where they should keep for up to a year.

Preparation

Lentils, unlike most other pulses, do not need to be soaked, but they should be washed thoroughly in a sieve under cold running water, and any damaged or discoloured ones discarded.

Cooking

Put one tablespoon of lentils into a small pot, add four tablespoons of filtered water and bring to the boil. Cover and simmer until soft and mushy. Remove lentils from cooking liquid and purée to a smooth texture using a blender. Any of the remaining cooking liquid can be used to get the right consistency. Lentils are best served with other vegetable purées such as potato, carrot, leek, etc.

Lettuce (from ten to twelve months)

Although lettuce can be introduced from six months. I would wait until your baby can eat it chopped up in a salad. This may not be until he is about a year old.

Health benefits

The most important nutrients in lettuce are folate and potassium.

Buying and storing

Choose lettuce with fresh bright-looking leaves. Avoid lettuces that show any signs of brown or yellow on the leaves.

Preparation

Never slice, cut or tear lettuce until you are ready to use it. When lettuce cells are torn they release ascorbic acid oxidase, an enzyme which destroys vitamin C.

Liver   (from eight to nine months)

Liver can be introduced in small amounts and can be surprisingly popular.

Health benefits
Liver is a very nutritious food for young babies and children. It is high in protein, iron, vitamins A and D, and the B vitamins.

Buying and storing
Choose lamb's liver that is dark-coloured and smells fresh. It should be washed under cold running water and dried with kitchen towel as soon as possible after purchasing. It can then be stored on a plate, loosely covered with foil and stored in the coolest part of the refrigerator. It should be used within two or three days of purchase.

Preparation
Wash under cold running water and dry on kitchen towel.

Cooking
Cut 50 g (2 oz) of lamb's liver into two pieces. Put in a pan, cover with freshly filtered water and bring to the boil. Cover, lower the heat and simmer until tender. Remove from cooking liquid and purée to a smooth texture in a blender. Any remaining cooking liquid can be used to achieve the right consistency.

Mangoes   (from five to six months)

Mango is an excellent food to introduce as a finger food to be eaten raw from six months. Before six months, it is advisable to cook it in a small amount of water to soften it enough. Baby rice served with mango purée is a great favourite with many babies.

Health benefits
Mangoes are a rich source of beta-carotene, which the body can convert to vitamin A. They also contain vitamin C.

Buying and storing

Choose ripe mangoes with smooth blemish-free skin that gives slightly when pressed. Ripe mangoes should be stored at a cool temperature or in the refrigerator, where they will keep for three to four days.

Preparation

Wash under cold running water, then cut around the middle of the fruit, which should allow you to prise the two sides apart from the stone. Cut the flesh into squares, then turn the fruit inside out. Slice the squares off the skin.

Cooking

Place ten to twelve squares in a pan and cover with just enough water to poach them until soft. They can then be mashed with a fork, or puréed in a blender to a smooth texture. Any remaining cooking liquid can be added to achieve the right consistency. From six months onwards, you won't need to cook the mango – simply cut off two or three slices and mash with a fork, or, for babies who are managing finger foods, cut into small bite-sized pieces.

Melon (from seven to eight months)

Melon is an excellent fruit to introduce when your baby is getting used to finger feeding. It is the right texture and needs no cooking.

Health benefits

Some varieties are good sources of beta carotene. Canteloupe and honeydew melons are good sources of vitamin C.

Buying and storing

Store at room temperature until ripe, thereafter in the refrigerator.

Preparation

Wash the melon under cold running water, cut in half and scoop out the seeds. Cut off as many slices as needed and trim off the skin. The remainder of the melon should be wrapped tightly in foil, stored in the refrigerator and eaten within one to two days. The melon that is to be used straight away should either be cut into bite-sized pieces, mashed with a fork, or puréed to a smooth texture in a blender.

Milk (from six months to one year)

Full-fat cow's milk (preferably organic) can be used in small amounts in cooking from the age of six months. It can replace formula or breast milk as a drink once your baby reaches one year. At one year of age your baby will need a minimum of 350ml (12oz) a day, inclusive of milk used in food, sauces, puddings, etc.

Health benefits

Milk is a source of high-quality protein and supplies vitamin A and essential B vitamins together with phosphorus. It is also an excellent source of calcium, which aids the formation of strong bones.

Buying and storing

Until your baby reaches two years of age he needs full-fat cow's milk. Whenever possible, buy organic cow's milk, and ensure that it is sealed when not in use and stored in the refrigerator. Never use milk that is past its sell-by date.

Preparation

By introducing your baby to cow's milk on his cereal and in puddings and sauces he should take to changing from formula or breast milk without any problems. If you do find that he refuses cow's milk to drink, try introducing it a little at a time mixed with formula or expressed breast milk. It can take a couple of weeks, but by increasing the ratio of cow's milk to formula he should reach a stage when he will happily take a full feed of cow's milk.

Cooking

Cow's milk can be used in cooking from six months. However, some nutritionists believe that the introduction of dairy products before one year can trigger allergies in children from allergic families. If you are thinking of avoiding dairy products because of allergy, please consult your GP or dietician.

Mushrooms (from eight to nine months)

In my experience babies either love or hate mushrooms. The best way to serve them is in a sauce or casserole.

Health benefits

Mushrooms are a good source of potassium and vitamin B_2 (riboflavin). They contain almost no fat.

Buying and storing

Choose small cream-coloured button mushrooms with smooth blemish-free skins. Larger flat mushrooms tend to be too strong-tasting for most babies. Store as for asparagus.

Preparation

Wash in a colander under cold running water, prior to cooking.

Cooking

Mushrooms for young babies are best cooked in a sauce or in casseroles.

Oats (from six months)

Oats, including unrefined rolled oatmeal cereal, can be introduced as a breakfast cereal from six months.

Health benefits

Oats contain high quantities of B vitamins and soluble fibre, which can help lower blood cholesterol. They are a good source of carbohydrate or starch, which is the body's main source of energy.

Buying and storing

Choose an unrefined oatmeal cereal that is specifically manufactured for young babies and fortified with extra vitamins and minerals. It should be additive- and gluten-free and have no sugars or fillers such as maltodextrin. Choose organic rolled oats in boxes or packets as opposed to cereal bought in bulk lots, which are much more likely to be exposed to contamination.

Oatmeal should be stored in a cool dry place. Most pre-packed cereals are in airtight boxes to avoid deterioration. If your packet of oatmeal cannot be sealed properly after each use, transfer to an airtight jar or container.

Preparation

Follow the manufacturer's instructions.

Cooking

The majority of first stage baby oatmeal rarely needs cooking. If you choose one that does, follow the manufacturer's instructions.

Parsnips (from five to six months)

Parsnips are another vegetable that young babies accept more readily if mixed with one or two other vegetables.

Health benefits

Parsnips are a useful source of beta carotene, folate and vitamin C. They are also high in potassium, phosphorus and iron.

Buying and storing

Choose small firm parsnips with unblemished creamy-coloured skins. Avoid larger parsnips as they are tough. Store as for green beans.

Preparation
Wash under cold running water, peel and slice.

Cooking
Parsnips should be put straight into the pan and covered with freshly filtered water the minute they are prepared to avoid them turning brown. Bring to the boil, cover, then lower the heat and simmer until tender. Remove from cooking liquid and purée to a smooth texture using a blender. Any remaining cooking liquid can be used to achieve the right consistency. Alternatively, formula or expressed milk can be used.

Pasta (from six to seven months)
There is a baby pasta available which does not need puréeing and this is often very popular. Adult pasta is best introduced when finger food is established.

Health benefits
Pasta is high in carbohydrates. These are very important for young babies and children as it provides them with energy.

Buying and storing
Choose organic wholemeal pasta that looks smooth and shiny. Store pasta in airtight containers.

Preparation
The preparation water should be boiling furiously before you add the pasta so that it can penetrate the pasta's starch granules as fast as possible.

Cooking
Pasta should be cooked in fast-boiling filtered water in a large saucepan. Add one tbsp oil to the water as this will help prevent the pasta sticking together.

Cooking time depends on the size of the pasta shapes: short pasta pieces will take six to twelve minutes, tiny pasta shapes two to six minutes and fresh home-made pasta about two to four minutes. Brands do vary enormously in the cooking time required, so always check the packet instructions.

Peaches (from five to six months)

Peaches are a great favourite with young babies and can be given before five months as a cooked purée. However, they can be quite fiddly and time-consuming to cook and purée, so I usually introduce them at six months, when they can be given raw.

Health benefits

Peaches are rich in vitamin C and fibre. They may also protect against cancer.

Buying and storing

Choose peaches that are firm to the touch and have a sweet smell. Store at a cool temperature or in the refrigerator where they will keep for two to four days.

Preparation

Wash under cold running water, then place in a bowl and cover with boiling water for one to two minutes, then straight into a bowl of cold water for one to two minutes. This will enable you to peel the peach easily. Cut the fruit into pieces, discarding the stone and pith. For babies over six months old the peach can be cut into bite-sized pieces and given raw.

Cooking

Place the peach in a pan, cover with a little water and poach until tender. Either mash with a fork or purée to a smooth texture using the remainder of the cooking liquid to achieve the right consistency.

Pears (from four to five months)

Pear is usually the first fruit that I give to babies as there are very few who dislike it or react badly to it, unlike apple or banana, which can sometimes cause constipation in certain babies when given with baby rice.

Health benefits
Pears are high in natural sugar and are sources of fibre and potassium. The vitamin C in pears is concentrated in the skin.

Buying and storing
Choose Comice pears or pears which are sweet and juicy. It is best to choose fruits that are firm, but slightly under-ripe with unblemished skin. This fruit tends to taste better if it is allowed to ripen in a cool room temperature. Once ripe, they will keep for a further two to three days in the refrigerator.

Preparation
Pears, like apples, tend to go brown the minute you peel or cut them. Therefore it is important to cook them as soon as they are prepared. Wash the pear under cold running water, quarter, peel off the skin and remove the core and any pith.

Cooking
Place the pear in a pot with just enough freshly filtered water to cover. Bring the pear and water to the boil, then cover with a lid, lower the heat and simmer until tender. Pears can be inclined to stick when cooking, so keep stirring throughout the cooking. Remove from the pan and either mash with a fork to a very smooth texture or purée in a blender. Any remaining cooking liquid can be used to achieve the right consistency.

From six months, it is not necessary to cook the pear – prepare as above, then mash or grate raw, directly onto food. Once your baby is ready for finger foods, it can be cut into bite-sized pieces.

Peas (from five to six months)

The majority of babies love the sweet taste of peas and provided your baby is not prone to bouts of wind, five to six months is a good time to introduce them in puréed form. Like other green vegetables, peas are best served with another vegetable such as sweet potato, parsnip, etc.

Health benefits

Peas are rich in vitamin B_1 (thiamine) and are a good source of vitamin C. They are a high protein food and a good source of beta carotene. They may be helpful against heart disease.

Buying and storing

Choose bright green firm, plump unblemished pods – small well-rounded pods usually provide sweeter peas. Peas should be stored loosely wrapped in a brown bag in the refrigerator and used within two to three days.

Preparation

Wash the pea pods in a colander under cold running water. Shell the peas into a bowl then wash again in the colander.

Cooking

Put the peas in a pan, bring to the boil, then lower the heat and just cover with freshly boiled filtered water. Bring to the boil, cover, then lower the heat and simmer until the peas are tender. Remove peas from the pan and purée to a very smooth texture, using any of the remaining cooking liquid to adjust the consistency.

Peppers (from six to seven months)

Peppers can be introduced in small amounts to vegetarian dishes and casseroles, and can be served raw in salads from approximately ten months.

Health benefits
Peppers are rich in vitamin C, which is essential for overall health. They are also a useful source of beta carotene.

Buying and storing
Choose firm brightly coloured peppers with blemish-free skins, that feel thick and fleshy to the touch. Peppers should be stored in the refrigerator to preserve their vitamin content.

Preparation
Wash under cold running water, cut into quarters and remove the seeds and pith, then dice or finely slice according to the recipe.

Cooking
Peppers can be chopped finely and fried before combining with other foods.

Pineapples (from nine to twelve months)
This is popular as a finger food, but can be puréed if your baby finds it difficult to chew.

Health benefits
Pineapples are a good source of vitamin C and manganese.

Buying and storing
Choose large firm blemish-free fruits with fresh-looking green leaves. The pineapple should feel heavy for its size, which is an indicator that it is juicy. Pineapples are best stored at room temperature and eaten when ripe.

Preparation
Wash the pineapple under cold running water, then turn it on its side and cut off the top, then one or two slices. Trim off the skin and cut out the eyes and the core, then cut into bite-sized cubes.

For babies whose chewing is not well developed put the pineapple cubes through a blender and purée to a smooth texture. The remainder of the pineapple should be tightly wrapped, stored in the refrigerator and used within a couple of days.

Plums (from seven to eight months)

If your baby is happily digesting a variety of different fruits it should be fine to introduce plums at this stage. I have had quite a few babies who have reacted badly to plums and therefore would advise you to introduce very small amounts to begin with.

Health benefits

Plums contain beta carotene and are a good source of potassium. They also contain small amounts of vitamins A, C and B.

Buying and storing

Choose firm but plump, brightly coloured fruits that yield slightly when pressed. Ripe plums should be loosely wrapped in a brown bag, stored in the refrigerator and used within two to three days.

Preparation

Wash the plums under cold running water, then place them in a bowl of boiling water for one to two minutes. Remove and place in a bowl of cold water until the skins split. Peel off the skin and remove the stones. The fruit can then be puréed to a smooth texture using a fork or a blender. For older babies who have mastered finger foods, they can be chopped into small bite-sized pieces.

Cooking

Place the prepared plums in a pan and cover with freshly filtered water. Bring to the boil and cover, then lower the heat and simmer until tender. Remove from the cooking liquid and purée to a smooth texture using a fork or a blender. Cooked puréed plums are ideal for serving with baby rice, custard or yoghurt.

Potatoes (from four to five months)

Potato is high in carbohydrates which are very important for young babies. Sweet potatoes are a particular favourite and an ideal choice to mix with other vegetables, particularly green vegetables.

Health benefits

Potatoes are a good source of vitamin C, potassium and fibre. Most of the vitamin C is found just underneath the skin, so try to cook and serve potatoes with the skins on. They are very high in carbohydrate or starch, and therefore provide lots of energy.

Buying and storing

Choose firm potatoes with blemish-free skin; avoid potatoes that have started to sprout or have green spots on them. Potatoes should ideally be stored in a cool dark airy cupboard to prevent them developing the green spots, which are toxic.

Preparation

Potatoes turn brown very quickly the minute they are cut, so they need to be prepared and cooked immediately. Cooking potatoes in their skins retains more vitamins and avoids this problem. Scrub the potato with a stiff vegetable brush under cold running water.

Cooking

Put in a pan and cover with cold filtered water. Bring to the boil and cover, then lower the heat and simmer until tender. Remove from the cooking liquid and allow the potato to cool slightly before peeling. Potatoes are best mashed to a very fine texture using a fork, then pressed through a sieve. The remainder of the cooking water can be used to adjust the consistency; alternatively, a small amount of formula or breast milk can be used.

Poultry (from six to seven months)

Chicken cooked on its own can be too strong-tasting for some babies. In my experience cooking it in a casserole with vegetables makes it much more palatable for a baby's first taste.

Health benefits

Chicken is usually the first animal protein that babies are given. It is a good source of the B vitamins, protein and iron.

Buying and storing

Oven-ready chickens are sold fresh or frozen, with or without giblets. They range in weight from 1.4 to 3.2 kg (3 to 7 lb). Pre-basted birds are also available. Corn-fed chicken has a distinctive yellow look and characteristic flavour because it is reared on a diet of maize. Chicken portions are avilable in many forms. In addition to chicken quarters, skinless, boneless breast fillets, thighs and drumsticks, look out for goujons (strips of breast meat). Poultry can contain low levels of salmonella and campylobactor – the bacteria that can cause food poisoning if they multiply, so raw chicken *must* be handled and stored hygienically. Always get poultry home and refrigerate as soon as possible after buying. If the bird contains giblets take them out and store in a separate container.

Preparation

Wash your hands before and after handling and never use the same utensils for preparing raw poultry and cooked food. If you buy frozen poultry, defrost it at cool room temperature rather than the fridge. Frozen food must be fully thawed before cooking.

Cooking

Always ensure poultry is cooked thoroughly. To test, pierce the thickest part of the thigh with a skewer. Only when the juices run clear – not at all pink – is the poultry cooked. Put leftover cooked poultry in the fridge as soon as it's cold and eat within two days.

Prunes (from eight to nine months)

These are best given when your baby is established on finger foods.

Health benefits

Prunes are a good source of the B vitamins and source of potassium and iron. They are a useful source of fibre and can relieve constipation.

Buying and storing

Some varieties are tenderised and do not need soaking, otherwise soak in filtered water or fruit juice. Store dried prunes in an airtight container.

Preparation

Most dried fruits need washing and soaking for at least three hours or overnight. However, some do not require soaking and come vacuum-packed and ready to eat. These can be kept sealed in the bag for future use.

Pulses (from seven to eight months)

Pulses, or dried beans, are an excellent form of vegetable protein but need to be served with another whole grain such as brown rice, wholewheat pasta, wholemeal bread, etc. if they are to replace a serving of animal protein. Apart from red lentils and butter beans, I have found that the majority of other pulses and dried beans are too difficult for young babies to digest and can cause wind. By seven months the majority of babies are established on three solid meals a day and should then be able to digest beans and pulses.

Health benefits

Beans are rich in carbohydrate and are a good source of protein and fibre. They are low in fat and contain B vitamins and folic acid. They can help control blood sugar and lower cholesterol levels.

Buying and storing

Choose smooth-skinned, uniformly sized, evenly coloured beans that are free of stones and debris. Check the use by date on the packet. Beans over one year old become tough and lose their flavour. Avoid beans sold in bulkas they may have been exposed to air and light and may have insect contamination (tiny holes in the bean indicate that an insect has burrowed into or through the bean). Store beans in airtight containers.

Preparation

Wash dried beans and pick them over carefully, discarding any damaged or withered beans and any that float. (Only withered beans are light enough to float in water.)

Cover the beans with filtered water, bring to the boil, and then set them aside to soak for 24 hours. When you are ready to use the beans, discard the water in which the beans have been soaked. Some of the indigestible sugars in the beans will leach out into the water, making the beans less gassy.

Cooking

Beans are best used in soups and stews.

Pumpkin (from seven to eight months)

Pumpkin soup is often a great favourite with babies.

Health benefits

Pumpkins are a good source of beta carotene and a useful source of vitamin E.

Buying and storing

Choose a pumpkin with bright orange blemish-free skin. You can also buy slices of pumpkin sold by weight.

Preparation

Cut the pumpkin in half and scoop out the seeds. Cut into sections and peel and chop the flesh into even-sized pieces.

Cooking

Cook the pumpkin in boiling filtered water for about 15 minutes or steam. Drain well and mash.

Spinach (from seven to eight months)

Introduce spinach with caution as some babies can have mild reactions. However, it is a vegetable that can be used in many meals.

Health benefits

Spinach is an excellent source of beta carotene and a good source of vitamin C, which may help prevent cancer. It is also a good source of potassium and folic acid. While spinach has a high content of iron, the oxalic acid in the leaves renders it unavailable.

Buying and storing

Choose fresh-looking spinach with dark-green blemish-free leaves. Store loosely wrapped in the refrigerator and use within two days.

Preparation

Wash the spinach leaves in filtered water several times as it collects dirt.

Cooking

Summer spinach should be steamed for three to four minutes in just the water that clings to the leaves. Winter spinach needs to have the stalks and central ribs removed before boiling in filtered water. Cook covered for five to ten minutes in a large saucepan. Drain well and press with the back of a wooden spoon. Serve either puréed or roughly chopped.

Swede and turnip (from four to five months)

Swede and turnip are ideal for mixing with other vegetables at the outset of weaning. They both go particularly well with potato and carrots.

Health benefits

Swede and turnip are good sources of vitamin C, beta carotene and fibre.

Buying and storing

Choose firm, well-formed small-to-medium swedes and turnips with blemish-free skins. Like potatoes, they are best stored unwashed in a cool dark airy cupboard where they will keep for up to two months. Stored at room temperature they would need to be used within a week.

Preparation

Scrub the swede or turnip under cold running water and cut off one or two slices approximately 1.25cm (½in) thick. Peel the skin off, then cut into cubes.

Cooking

Place the swede or turnip in a pan just covered with freshly filtered water. Bring to the boil, cover, then lower the heat and simmer until tender. Remove from the cooking liquid and purée to a smooth texture using a blender. Any remaining cooking liquid can be used to adjust the purée to the right consistency.

Tomatoes (from seven to eight months)

Health benefits

Tomatoes are medium in sugar but have no starch. They are an excellent source of vitamin C and a good source of potassium. They are best served fresh and ripe.

Buying and storing

Choose smooth, round or oval tomatoes. The tomatoes should feel heavy for their size; their flesh should be firm, not watery. If you plan to use them immediately, pick ripe ones whose skin is a deep orange/red colour. If you plan to store the tomatoes for a few days, pick tomatoes whose skin is still slightly yellow or pink. Avoid bruised tomatoes or tomatoes with mould around the stem end. The damaged tomatoes may be rotten inside; the mouldy ones may be contaminated with mycotoxins (poisons produced by moulds).

Preparation

Remove and discard all the stalks and leaves – they are poisonous. Wash the tomatoes under cool running water, then slice and serve. Alternatively, peel the tomatoes by plunging them into boiling water, then transferring them on a slotted spoon into a bowl of cold water. The change in temperature damages a layer of cells just under the skin so that the skins slips off easily. To get rid of the seeds, cut the tomato in half across the middle and squeeze the two halves gently, cut side down, over a bowl. The seeds should pop out easily.

Vegetable oils (from seven to eight months)

Health benefits

Vegetable oils are our best source of vitamin E. Best used only once and certainly not after repeated use in a chip fryer.

Buying and storing

Choose tightly sealed bottles of vegetable oil, protected from light and heat.

Yoghurt (from six to seven months)

Health benefits

Yoghurt, like all milk products, is a good source of thiamine (vitamin B_1) and riboflavin (vitamin B_2). It is also a good source of calcium.

Buying and storing

Choose tightly sealed, refrigerated containers. Check the date on the container to buy the freshest product.

Preparation

Do not 'whip' yoghurt before adding it to any dish; you will break the curd and make the yoghurt watery.

Useful Addresses

Baby equipment
The Great Little Trading Company
124 Walcot Street
Bath BA1 5BG
Tel: 0870 241 4082

Cooking equipment
Little plastic pots, containers for freezing meals in bulk as well as a range of food processors are available from all John Lewis Partnership stores throughout the UK.

Suppliers of organic produce
The Soil Association provides information about deliveries of organic vegetables in your area.
Tel: 01179 290 661
To order their full organic shopping catalogue:
Tel: 01179 142 446

The Fresh Food Company offers a home delivery service of organic vegetables, meat, fish, game, dairy produce and bread nationwide.
Tel: 020 8969 0351

Telephone consultations and advice
Contact Gina Ford on 01289 303351. Or visit her new website: www.contentedbaby.com

Further Reading

The New Contented Little Baby Book by Gina Ford (Vermilion, 1999)

From Contented Baby to Confident Child by Gina Ford (Vermilion, 2000)

The Food Our Children Eat by Joanna Blythman (Fourth Estate, 1999)

Annabel Karmel's New Complete Baby and Toddler Meal Planner (Ebury Press, 1998)

Annabel Karmel's Superfoods for Babies and Children (Ebury Press, 2001)

Planet Organic: Baby & Toddler Cookbook by Lizzie Vann (Dorling Kindersley, 2000)

Optimum Nutrition for Babies & Young Children by Lucy Burney (Piatkus, 1999)

Good First Foods by Sara Lewis (Hamlyn, 2002)

Index